THE DIARY OF ANNE FRANK

In Two Acts

Dramatized by

FRANCES GOODRICH

and

ALBERT HACKETT

from the book
ANNE FRANK: DIARY OF A YOUNG GIRL

SAMUEL   FRENCH

LONDON
NEW YORK TORONTO SYDNEY HOLLYWOOD

THE DIARY OF ANNE FRANK

THE DIARY OF ANNE FRANK

Produced at the Phoenix Theatre, London, on the 29th November 1956, with the following cast of characters—

(in the order of their appearance)

Mr Frank	*George Voskovec*
Miep Gies	*Jane Jordan Rogers*
Mrs Van Daan	*Miriam Karlin*
Mr Van Daan	*Max Bacon*
Peter Van Daan	*Harry Lockart*
Mrs Frank	*Vera Fusek*
Margot Frank	*Clarissa Stolz*
Anne Frank	*Perlita Neilson*
Mr Kraler	*Kynaston Reeves*
Mr Dussel	*John Gabriel*

Directed by Frith Banbury
Setting by Boris Aronson

SYNOPSIS OF SCENES

The action of the play passes in the top floors of a warehouse in Amsterdam, Holland

ACT I

Scene 1	November 1945.	Late afternoon
Scene 2	July 1942.	Early morning
Scene 3	August 1942.	A few minutes after 6 p.m.
Scene 4	September 1942.	Midnight
Scene 5	December 1942.	Night

ACT II

Scene 1	January 1944.	Late afternoon
Scene 2	March 1944.	Evening
Scene 3	April 1944.	Night
Scene 4	July 1944.	Afternoon
Scene 5	November 1945.	Late afternoon

NOTES

EVERYONE on the stage is in view at all times. The people in a scene move about enough to seem natural, but their movements are never fast or sudden or so unusual as to attract attention.

Although each of the Acts is divided into five scenes, there should be a flow, making the Act seem like one scene. This is accomplished by cross-fading lights and the sound at the beginning and end of each scene. The one exception to this method is between II-4 and II-5—there are several seconds of deliberate silence in the black-out after "some day I hope . . ." The black drop for scene changes should not be seen coming in or going out.

The bag of potatoes used by MR DUSSEL in II-3 are baked for easy handling and to avoid their rolling around.

It is possible to eliminate the platform in the centre room, leaving ANNE's and PETER's rooms on platforms. Hers about one foot high, his about three feet six inches. The stairs going down can be eliminated by making a tunnel under PETER's room. This tunnel should be about three feet high by two feet six inches wide, with a door opening on stage. All enter on hands and knees.

It is also possible to eliminate the attic room if necessary, and have the stairs lead to a platform off L.

PRONUNCIATIONS

Amen, Oh-mein
Amsterdam, Ahm'-ster-dahm
Anne, Ah'-nah or the familiar Ah'-nee
Anneke, Ah'nah-kah
Anneline, Ah-nah-lynn
Auschwitz, Aow'-shvitz
Belsen, Bell'-sen
Buchenwald, Buch'-en-vald
Delphi, Dell'-fie
Dirk, Dee'-urk
Dussel, Duss'-ell
Edith, Ae'-dit
Frank, Frahnk
Hallensteins, Ha'-len-stains
Hilversum, Hill'-ver-sum
Jan, Yan
Jopie, Yo'-pee

Kerli, Care'-lee
Kraler, Krah'-ler
Liefje, Leaf'-yah
Margot, Mar'-gott
Mauthausen, Maut'-how-sen
Mazeltov, Mah'-zel-tahv
Miep, Meep
Mouschi, Moo'-shee
Otto, Ah'-toe
Peter, Pay'-ter
Petronella, Pet-row-nell'-ah
Putti, Poo'-tee
Rotterdam, Rah'-ter-dahm
Van Daan, Fahn Dahn
Wessels, Vess'-ells
Westertoren, Vess'-ter-tor-en
Wilhelmina, Vil-hel-mee'-nah

THE DIARY OF ANNE FRANK

ACT I

SCENE 1

SCENE—*The top floors of a warehouse in Amsterdam, Holland. November 1945. Late afternoon.*

The sharply peaked roof of the building is outlined against a sea of other rooftops, stretching away in the distance. Nearby is the belfry of a church tower, the Westertoren, whose carillon rings out the hours. The three rooms of the top floor and a small attic space above are exposed to our view. The largest of the rooms is in the centre, with two small rooms, slightly raised, on either side. The area is cramped and inhospitable. Unfinished plaster walls are cracked and crumbling, stained wallpaper is fading on some walls and raw bricks are exposed beneath. Heavy naked beams cut through the centre room. In the room R, a chaise-longue, with legs removed, rests on the floor parallel to the curtain line. Its head is R against the wall. At its foot is a low wooden box that extends the length of this bed. Immediately upstage in the wall R is a window and window-seat. The lid of this seat may be raised. The window is covered with a two-ply, dark brown, blackout curtain. The wall jogs towards the centre at the upstage edge of the window and on this wall face are seven wooden pegs. The wall up R is covered with many pictures and photographs, drawing-pinned in place. Queen Wilhelmina, a small map of Holland, Shirley Temple, Garbo, Robert Taylor, are in the collection. A cot has been placed along this side with its head against the rear wall. C of the rear wall we see a window with dirty, frosted panes. Under the window is a low chest of drawers. The wall L consists only of the door flat, up L. This door has two panes of glass that have been painted over, and it is hinged on the upstage edge to swing into the main room. Two steps, inside the door, lead up into the room. There is a pipe-frame washstand downstage of the door against what would be the wall L. It is used as a dressing-table. A lamp with a small opaque shade, a small standing mirror, hairbrush, comb, etc. are on this table. Two chamber vessels are visible; one under the cot, the other under the washstand. At the foot of the cot is a wooden box with a sewing basket on it, and a bulb with a frosted glass shade hangs from the ceiling above. This light is controlled by a switch downstage on the door frame. Down R in the centre room, with its back flush against the diagonal cut of the platform that is the room R, is a small armless couch. It is constructed so that a shelf may be pulled out from the base, forming a second sleeping space. Above the left end of the couch is a battered table with a small lamp on it. The room is sparsely furnished; a rectangular table is C; there are two ladder-backed chairs with wicker seats, two mismated chairs with wooden arms and upholstered seats, and a footstool with a

1

*padded top. Immediately above the door to the room R, three steps rise
to a small door which swings offstage and leads to the W.C. When the
W.C. light is on, it can be seen shining dimly through the window in
the back wall of the room R. The remainder of the wall up R consists of
a fireplace with a rough wooden mantelpiece. On the downstage end of
the mantelpiece is a small lamp. The opening of the fireplace has been
plastered over but contains a sleeve to admit the pipe of a small,
cylindrical, iron heating stove that stands in front of it. The top of this
stove has a single, removable "lid" such as is found on old wood-
burning cooking stoves. At the up R corner of the room, parallel to the
footlights, is the kitchen area. A sink with a single, practical tap is
in the up R corner. The draining-board extends L and a two-burner gas
hotplate has been placed on it. The wall above holds a shelf and hanging
rack. There are pots, pans, skillets, and various utensils in evidence.
Under the sink is a cupboard with two doors, which is used as a food
chest. Upstage and behind the kitchen is a narrow curtained opening
going off R. Up C, in the rear wall, is another large window, which has
been boarded over. Only a small area in the upper left corner remains
clear. By standing on the first step of the stairs which run off up L, a
person can peer out. This flight of narrow steps leads up to the attic
room. The upstage section of the wall L is recessed and has four shelves
built into it. Here is kept china, glassware, linen, medicine, brandy, an
iron, etc. At the upstage end of these shelves are three hooks from which
clothes may be hung. At LC is the door to the room L. It is hinged
upstage and opens into the centre room. Downstage of this door is a
short flight of stairs leading down to a door that is hinged upstairs and
swings on. When open, we can see the bookcase that camouflages the
entrance from the office below. The handrail is upstage. This stair-
well runs under the platform of the room L. The room L is supported in
such a way that the audience can see down the stair-well to the door
beneath. At C, hanging from the beam that is the supporting member
under the attic room, hangs a bulb with a heavy metal shade slung under
it. This shade is perforated to permit some direct light to shine through,
but is primarily indirect in function. A wire is stretched, above head
height, from the downstage edge of the shelf area up L, across the room
to just below the sink. Two crude curtains of faded material hang from
rings on this wire. If extended they would conceal the sink, staircase and
shelf area from the remainder of the room. These curtains are usually
pushed well open. Inside the room L two steps lead up to a platform
level. As you enter, a curtain upstage conceals a closet area. Downstage
is another step that leads up to the bedroom level. Along what would be
the wall R, a bed has been constructed by putting a mattress on a door,
supported by two boxes. A skylight, set at an angle, is down L and the
wall upstage of it jogs diagonally onstage. This angular area contains
another rise in the platform that gives the effect of an irregular window-
seat. At LC a fruit crate stands on end against the wall. It is used as a
small table and storage space. A brass, goose-necked lamp is on the
window-seat, and a blackout curtain of brown material is hanging*

below the skylight. The curtain can be lifted and hooked at the top edge of the sash to cover the dusty panes. The attic stair-well opens into the extreme up L *corner of the attic room. Down* L *are several cardboard cartons, a small packing case, etc. Back* C *is a wardrobe built into the wall. A brass bed is down* R, *with the headboard* R, *extending onstage. A person can move above the bed and get off* R *out of the audience's view. A wall lamp with a glass shade is* R *of the wardrobe, and a small wooden stool is* C *at the foot of the bed.*

(See the Ground Plan and Photograph of the Scene)

When the CURTAIN *rises, the stage is in darkness.*

Lighting Cue 1

The LIGHTS *come slowly up on the back-cloth, revealing the rooftops and belfry tower. Gradually the light in the rooms follows. The last fading rays of the sun come weakly through the skylight. The living area is in disarray, implying those who live here made a hasty exit. In the room* R *we can see the covering of the chaise is worn and faded. The cot has been stripped of covering, leaving the mattress exposed. The mirror is face down on the dressing-table and no lamp is in evidence. The door is closed. In the centre room the couch has a split in its back where springs and stuffing have broken through. There is no lamp on the table* R. *The padded footstool stands above the table* R. *A large map of the war area hangs over the fireplace. Up* R, *the curtain sags limply, concealing most of the kitchen area. A tattered curtain covers the window up* C. *The dividing curtain* L *is also extended. It has fallen to shreds with the passage of time, and partially conceals an upright chair overturned behind it. One armchair is* L, *just above the stair-well. A ball of yarn and knitting needles have been left on it. Down* L, *the other armchair has been thrown over. The table* C *is overturned, and* R *of it, the other upright chair lies on its side. An inexpertly knitted, multi-coloured scarf hangs upstage of the door* L. *A woman's white glove is on the floor by the table* R. *The room* L *is bare, the door ajar. A withered plant droops from a pot on the window-seat. The bed is stripped, the mattress exposed.*

Effects Cue 1

As the lights approach full, we hear the melody of the carillon chiming before the hour.

Effects Cue 2

As the carillon fades, the sound of ships' sirens are heard in the distance. After a moment the door at the foot of the stair-well swings open and MR FRANK *enters up the stairs. He is a gentle, cultured European in his middle years. There is a trace of a German accent in his speech. He is weak and ill and is making a supreme effort at self-control. His clothes are threadbare. He carries a small rucksack.*

Effects Cue 3

As he reaches the top of the stairs, the chimes strike six o'clock. MR FRANK *moves slowly across to the couch, where he puts down his rucksack, and then moves up* R.

Effects Cue 4

We can hear children outside begin a gay song as they play, and a street organ begins its jaunty air. Mr Frank *opens the door* R, *peers in, then closes the door and moves restlessly up* C. *The scarf catches his eye. He takes it down, puts it around his neck, then wanders towards the couch, but stops as he sees the glove. He picks it up. Suddenly all control is gone. He breaks down and weeps.* Miep Gies *enters up the stairs. She is a Dutch girl of about twenty-two, pregnant now. She gives one a feeling of great capacity and courage. She is compassionate and protective in her attitude towards Mr Frank. She has been a stenographer and secretary in his business. She has her coat and hat on, ready to go home. A small silver cross hangs at her throat.*

Miep (*as she comes up the stairs*) Are you all right, Mr Frank?

Mr Frank (*quickly controlling himself*) Yes, Miep, yes.

Miep. Everyone in the office has gone home—it's after six. (*She moves and stands above the table. Pleading*) Don't stay up here, Mr Frank. What's the use of torturing yourself like this?

Mr Frank. I've come to say good-bye—I'm leaving here, Miep.

Miep. What do you mean? Where are you going? Where?

Mr Frank. I don't know yet. I haven't decided.

Miep. Mr Frank, you can't leave here. This is your home. Amsterdam is your home.

(Mr Frank *crosses restlessly above Miep to* L *of her*)

Your business is here, waiting for you. You're needed here. Now that the war is over, there are things that . . .

Mr Frank. I can't stay in Amsterdam, Miep. It has too many memories for me. Everywhere there's something—the house we lived in—the school—the street organ playing out there. (*He moves wearily down* L) I'm not the person you used to know, Miep. I'm a bitter old man. (*He breaks off and returns to* L *of Miep*) Forgive me. I shouldn't speak to you like this—after all that you did for us—the suffering . . .

Miep. No. No. It wasn't suffering. (*She straightens a chair* L *of the table, which is overturned*) You can't say we suffered.

Mr Frank. I know what you went through, you and Mr Kraler. I'll remember it as long as I live. (*He gives one last look round then moves towards the stairs*) Come, Miep. (*He remembers his rucksack, crosses below the table to the couch and picks up his rucksack*)

Miep (*hurrying to the shelves up* L) Mr Frank, did you see? There are some of your papers here. (*She takes a bundle of papers from the shelves, then crosses below the table to Mr Frank*) We found them in a heap of rubbish on the floor after—after you left.

Mr Frank. Burn them. (*He opens his rucksack and puts the glove in it*)

Miep. But, Mr Frank, there are letters, notes . . .

Mr Frank. Burn them. All of them.

Miep. Burn this? (*She hands him a worn, velour-covered book*)

Mr Frank (*quietly*) Anne's diary. (*He opens the diary and reads*) "Monday, the sixth of July, nineteen hundred and forty-two." (*To Miep*) Nineteen hundred and forty-two. Is it possible, Miep? Only three years ago. (*He reads*) "Dear Diary, since you and I are going to be great friends, I will start by telling you about myself. My name is Anne Frank. I am thirteen years old." (*He sits on the couch*) "I was born in Germany the twelfth of June, nineteen twenty-nine. As my family is Jewish, we emigrated to Holland when Hitler came to power."

(*As* Mr Frank *reads on, another* Voice *joins his, fading slowly in, as if coming from the air. It is* Anne's Voice)

Mr Frank }(*together*)
Anne's Voice}

"My father started a business, importing spice and herbs. Things went well for us until nineteen forty. Then the War came and the Dutch—(*he turns the page*) defeat, followed by the arrival of the Germans."

Lighting Cue 2

(*The* Lights *start to fade except for a spot focused on Mr Frank and Miep*)

"Then things got very bad for the Jews."

(Mr Frank's *voice dies out as* Anne's Voice *grows stronger*)

Anne. You could not do this and you could not do that.

Lighting Cue 3

(*The spot on Mr Frank and Miep fades*)

They forced father out of his business. We had to wear yellow stars. I had to turn in my bike. I couldn't go to a Dutch school any more. I couldn't go to the cinema, or ride in an automobile, or even on a streetcar, and a million other things. But somehow we children still managed to have fun. Yesterday, father told me we were going into hiding. Where, he wouldn't say. At five o'clock this morning mother woke me and told me to hurry and get dressed. I was to put on as many clothes as I could. It would look too suspicious if we walked along carrying suitcases. It wasn't until we were on our way that I learned where we were going. Our hiding place was to be upstairs in the building where father used to have his business.

Lighting Cue 4

(*The* Lights *come slowly up. Simultaneously* Anne's Voice *begins to fade*)

Three other people were coming in with us—the Van Daans and

their son Peter. Father knew the Van Daans but we had never met them.

Effects Cue 5

(*The sound of distant ships' sirens are heard*)

SCENE 2

SCENE—*The same. Early morning, July 1942.*

The photographs we saw at first, the war map, the dead plant and the knitting are not there. The rooms have been prepared for living. All the beds are made, the lamps are in place and the furniture upright. The table c *is flanked by an upright chair* L *and an armchair* R. *The other upright chair is up* R, *above the stove. The dividing curtains are partially drawn, and although far from new, are not in shreds.*

When the LIGHTS *come up, the three members of the* VAN DAAN *family are waiting for the Franks to arrive.* MR VAN DAAN *is pacing up* c, *smoking a cigarette and watching his wife with a nervous eye. His overcoat and suit are expensive and well-cut.* MRS VAN DAAN *is sitting on the couch. She is a pretty woman in her early forties and is clutching her possessions; a hat-box, a handbag and an attractive straw carry-all. A cardboard carton, tied with a heavy cord, is beside her on the seat of the couch.* PETER VAN DAAN *is standing at the window in the room* R, *looking down at the street below. He is a shy, awkward boy of sixteen. He wears a cap, a short overcoat, and long Dutch trousers, like "plus fours". At his feet is a black carrier with a cat in it and on the window-seat he has stood a small potted plant. All the* VAN DAANS *have the conspicuous yellow Star of David on the left breast of their clothing. As the lights reach full,* MRS VAN DAAN *sneezes.* MR VAN DAAN *glances at her, looks at his watch, then moves* L *and puts out his cigarette.* MRS VAN DAAN *rises, nervous and excited, and moves below the table* c.

MRS VAN DAAN. Something's happened to them. I know it.

MR VAN DAAN (*moving to her*) Now, Kerli!

MRS VAN DAAN. Mr Frank said they'd be here at seven o'clock. He said . . .

MR VAN DAAN. They have two miles to walk. You can't expect . . .

MRS VAN DAAN (*overlapping*) They've been picked up.

(*The door below opens*)

That's what's happened. They've been taken.

(MR VAN DAAN *indicates that he hears someone coming*)

MR VAN DAAN. You see?

(MR FRANK *comes up the stair-well from below. He looks much younger now. His movements are brisk and his manner confident. He wears an overcoat and carries his hat and a small cardboard box*)

MR FRANK. Mrs Van Daan, Mr Van Daan. (*He crosses to the Van Daans and shakes hands with them*)

(PETER *picks up his cat carrier and small plant, comes into the centre room and stands by the door* R. MRS VAN DAAN *moves to the couch*)

(*He moves to Peter and shakes his hand, then puts his box on the table and moves down* RC) There were too many of the Green Police on the streets—we had to take the long way round.

(MIEP, *not pregnant now,* MARGOT, MR KRALER, *and* MRS FRANK *come up the stairs.* MARGOT *is eighteen, beautiful, quiet and shy. She carries a leatherette hold-all and a large brown paper bag, which she puts on the table.* KRALER *is a Dutchman, dependable and kindly. He wears a hearing aid in his ear and carries two brief-cases.* MRS FRANK *is a young mother, gently bred and reserved. She, like Mr Frank, has a slight German accent. She carries a leatherette shopping bag and her handbag. We see the Star of David conspicuous on the Franks' clothing.* KRALER *acknowledges the Van Daans, moves to the shelves up* L *and checks their contents.* MIEP *and* MARGOT *move above the table* C. MIEP *empties her straw bag of the clothes it contains and piles them on the right end of the table*)

MRS FRANK (*calling down the stairs*)   Anne?

(ANNE FRANK *comes quickly up the stairs. She is thirteen, quick in her movements, interested in everything and mercurial in her emotions. She wears a cape, long wool socks and carries a school bag*)

MR FRANK (*moving* C *below the table*)   My wife, Edith. Mr and Mrs Van Daan.

(MRS FRANK *shakes Mr Van Daan's hand, then hurries across to shake hands with Mrs Van Daan. She then moves to the sink and inspects it*)

Their son, Peter—my daughters, Margot and Anne.

(ANNE *gives a polite little curtsy as she shakes Mr Van Daan's hand. She puts her bag on the left end of the table* C *then immediately starts off on a tour of investigation of her new home, going upstairs to the attic room.* MR VAN DAAN *sits* L *of the table and fans himself.* MIEP *takes a thermos of milk from the bag on the table and puts it on the draining-board*)

KRALER (*crossing above the table to Mr Frank*)   I'm sorry there is still so much confusion.

MR FRANK. Please. Don't think of it. After all, we'll have plenty of leisure to arrange everything ourselves.

(KRALER *goes into the room* R *and places his brief-cases on the floor by the dressing-table*)

MIEP (*indicating the sink cupboard*) We put the stores of food you sent in here. (*She crosses to the shelves up* L) Your drugs are here—soap, linen, here.

(MR FRANK *goes to the mantelpiece, puts his hat on it, then crosses to the shelves up* L. MRS FRANK *moves to the shelves.* MARGOT *takes the bag of food from the table and puts the items into the sink cupboard*)

MRS FRANK. Thank you, Miep.

MIEP. I made up the beds—the way Mr Frank and Mr Kraler said.

(KRALER, *having inspected the room* R, *comes into the centre room and goes to the couch*)

(*She hurries towards the stair-well*) Forgive me. I have to hurry. I've got to go to the other side of town to get some ration books for you.

MRS VAN DAAN (*rising*) Ration books? If they see our names on ration books, they'll know we're here.

KRALER ⎱ (*together*) ⎰ There isn't anything . . .

MIEP ⎰   ⎱ Don't worry. Your names won't be on them. (*As she hurries out*) I'll be up later.

MR FRANK (*crossing to the stair-well and watching Miep leave*) Thank you, Miep.

(MIEP *exits down the stair-well*)

MRS FRANK (*crossing to Kraler; troubled*) It's illegal, then, the ration books? We've never done anything illegal.

MR FRANK. We won't be living exactly according to regulations here.

(KRALER *moves to Mrs Frank, takes several small bottles of medicine from his coat pockets and gives them to her*)

KRALER (*reassuringly*) This isn't the black market, Mrs Frank. This is what we call the white market—helping all of the hundreds and hundreds who are hiding out in Amsterdam.

Effects Cue 6

(*The carillon is heard playing the quarter hour before eight.* KRALER *looks at his watch.* ANNE *comes down from the attic, stops at the window and looks out through the curtains*)

ANNE. It's the Westertoren.

KRALER. I must go. (*He shakes hands with Peter and Mrs Van Daan*)

(ANNE *inspects the kitchen area.* MARGOT *stands above the table*)

I must be out of here and downstairs in the office before the

workmen get here. Miep or I, or both of us, will be up each day
to bring you food and news and find out what your needs are.

(MR FRANK *crosses to the stair-well and waits by it for Kraler*)

Tomorrow I'll get you a better bolt for the door at the foot of
the stairs. It needs a bolt that you can throw yourself and open
only at our signal. (*To Mr Frank*) Oh—you'll tell them about
the noise?

MR FRANK. I'll tell them.

KRALER. Good-bye, then, for the moment. I'll come up again,
after the workmen leave.

MR FRANK (*shaking Kraler's hand*) Good-bye, Mr Kraler.

MRS FRANK (*shaking Kraler's hand*) How can we thank you?

KRALER. I never thought I'd live to see the day when a
man like Mr Frank would have to go into hiding. When you
think . . .

(KRALER *breaks off and exits down the stairs. MR FRANK
follows him down the stairs and bolts the door after him. In the interval
before he returns,* PETER *goes to Margot, gives a stiff bow and shakes
hands with her.* ANNE, *up* C, *watches, and as they complete their
greeting, moves to Peter and holds out her hand.* PETER *does not see her
and turns away.* MRS FRANK *drifts thoughtfully up* L. MR FRANK
comes up the stairs)

MRS FRANK (*hurrying to Mr Frank*) What did he mean, about
the noise?

MR FRANK. First, let's take off some of these clothes. (*He
crosses to the chair above the iron stove and places his overcoat on it*)

(ANNE *moves below the table, stands with her back to the audience,
removes her cape and beret and puts them on the pile of clothes on the
table. They all start to take off garment after garment. On each of their
coats, sweaters, blouses, suits and dresses is another yellow Star of
David.* MR *and* MRS FRANK *are under-dressed quite simply. The
others wear several things, sweaters, extra dresses, bathrobes, aprons,
etc.* MRS FRANK *takes off her gloves, carefully folding them before
putting them away*)

MR VAN DAAN (*crossing to the couch*) It's a wonder we weren't
arrested, walking along the streets—Petronella with a fur coat
in July—and that cat of Peter's crying all the way.

ANNE (*removing a pair of panties*) A cat?

MRS FRANK (*shocked*) Anne, please!

ANNE. It's all right. I've got on three more (*She removes two
more pairs of panties*)

(MR FRANK *crosses above the table and stands down* L. *Finally, as
they finish removing their surplus clothes, they settle down.* MRS
FRANK *sits* L *of the table.* ANNE *sits on the table, feet dangling.*
MARGOT *stands above the table.* MR *and* MRS VAN DAAN *sit on*

the couch. PETER is by the door R where he has placed his clothes on the stool)

MR FRANK. Now. About the noise. While the men are in the building below, we must have complete quiet. Every sound can be heard down there, not only in the workrooms, but in the offices, too. The men come about eight-thirty, and leave at about five-thirty. So, to be perfectly safe, from eight in the morning until six in the evening we must move only when it is necessary and then in stockinged feet. (*He crosses below the table to* RC) We must not speak above a whisper. We must not run any water. We cannot use the sink, or even, forgive me, the W.C. The pipes go down through the workrooms. It would be heard. No rubbish . . .

Effects Cue 7

(*The sound of marching feet is heard off.* MR FRANK *goes into the room* R, *followed by* ANNE, *and peers out of the window. Satisfied that the marching feet are going away, he returns and continues.* ANNE *follows him and curls up in the chair* R *of the table*)

No rubbish must ever be thrown out which might reveal that someone is living here—not even a potato paring. We must burn everything in the stove at night. This is the way we must live until it is over, if we are to survive. (*He moves* R)

(*There is a pause.* MARGOT *accidentally drops the nightgown she is taking off.* PETER *jumps to pick it up for her, then crosses and stands above the left end of the table*)

MRS FRANK. Until it is over.

MR FRANK. After six we can move about—we can talk and laugh and have our supper and read and play games—just as we would at home. (*He looks at his watch*) And now I think it would be wise if we all went to our rooms, and were settled before eight o'clock. Mrs Van Daan, you and your husband will go upstairs. I regret that there's no place up there for Peter. But he will be here, near us. This will be our common room, where we'll meet to talk and eat and read, like one family.

MRS VAN DAAN. And where do you and Mrs Frank sleep?

MR FRANK. This room is also our bedroom.

(MRS VAN DAAN *rises in protest and crosses to Mr Frank, carrying her coat, hatbox and straw bag*)

MRS VAN DAAN } (*together*) { That isn't right. We'll sleep here
MR VAN DAAN } { and you take the room upstairs. It's your place.

MR FRANK. Please. I've thought this out for weeks. It's the best arrangement. The only arrangement.

(Mr Van Daan *starts to load his arms with the clothes he and his wife have taken off and thrown across the couch*)

Mrs Van Daan (*shaking Mr Frank's hand*)   Never, never can we thank you. (*She moves to Mrs Frank and shakes her hand*) I don't know what would have happened to us, if it hadn't been for Mr Frank.

Mr Frank. You don't know how your husband helped me when I came to this country—knowing no-one—not able to speak the language. I can never repay him for that. (*He moves to Van Daan*) May I help you with your things?

Mr Van Daan. No. No. (*He picks up the carton and moves towards the attic stairs. To Mrs Van Daan*) Come along, liefje.

Mrs Van Daan. You'll be all right, Peter? You're not afraid?

Peter (*embarrassed*)   Please, Mother. (*He crosses to* R *and picks up his gear*)

(Mrs Frank *goes to the head of the stair-well and stares thoughtfully down.* Mr *and* Mrs Van Daan *go upstairs*)

Mr Frank (*moving above the table*) You, too, must have some rest, Edith. You didn't close your eyes last night. Nor you Margot.

Anne. I slept, Father. Wasn't that funny? I knew it was the last night in my own bed, and yet I slept soundly.

(Peter *carries his gear across and places it on the chair below the door* L, *setting the cat case on the floor*)

Mr Frank. I'm glad, Anne. Now you'll be able to help me straighten things in here. (*To Mrs Frank and Margot*) Come with me—you and Margot rest in this room for the time being. (*He opens the door of the room* R)

Mrs Frank (*crossing above the table to Mr Frank*) You're sure? I could help, really. And Anne hasn't had her milk.

Mr Frank. I'll give it to her. (*He crosses to the table and picks up the pile of clothes. To Anne and Peter*) Anne, Peter—it's best that you take off your shoes now, before you forget. (*He leads the way to the room* R, *goes in and switches on the pendant light*)

Lighting Cue 5

(Margot *goes into the room* R, *taking her bag with her.* Anne *and* Peter *remove their shoes*)

Mrs Frank. You're sure you're not tired, Anne?

Anne. I feel fine. I'm going to help father.

Mrs Frank. Peter, I'm glad you are to be with us.

Peter. Yes, Mrs Frank.

(Mrs Frank *goes into the room* R *and closes the door. During the following scene* Mr Frank *helps* Margot *to hang up the clothes he has piled on the cot up* R. *Coats and hats are put in the window seat.*

Skirts, sweaters and blouses are hung on the peg above the window. He takes a pillow from the chest for Margot's bed and puts the remainder of the clothes into the drawer. He then moves Kraler's brief-cases and puts them with Margot's bag below the dressing-table. MARGOT *puts her comb and brush, etc. on the dressing-table, then lies down on the cot up* R. MRS FRANK *carefully folds her things on the box at the foot of the bed down* R, *then lies on it. All this is unhurried.* PETER *takes his cat out of its case*)

ANNE (*crossing to Peter*) What's your cat's name?

PETER (*self-conscious and shy*) "Mouschi".

ANNE (*to the cat*) Mouschi! Mouschi! Mouschi! (*She picks up the cat, goes up* L, *circles the table and finishes below it*) I love cats. I have one—a darling little cat. But they made me leave her behind. I left some food and a note for the neighbours to take care of her—I'm going to miss her terribly. What is yours? A him or a her?

PETER (*crossing to* L *of her*) He's a tom. He doesn't like strangers. (*He takes the cat from Anne, crosses and puts it back in its carrier*)

ANNE (*moving to Peter; unabashed*) Then I'll have to stop being a stranger, won't I? Is he fixed?

PETER (*startled*) Huh?

ANNE. Did you have him altered?

PETER. No.

ANNE. Oh, you ought to—to keep him from fighting. Where did you go to school?

PETER. Jewish Secondary.

ANNE. But that's where Margot and I go. I never saw you around.

PETER. I used to see you—sometimes.

ANNE. You did?

PETER. In the school yard. You were always in the middle of a bunch of kids. (*He takes a penknife from his pocket*)

ANNE. Why didn't you ever come over?

PETER. I'm sort of a lone wolf. (*He starts to rip off his Star of David*)

ANNE. What are you doing?

PETER. Taking it off.

ANNE. But you can't do that. (*She grabs his hands and stops him*) They'll arrest you if you go out without your star.

PETER (*pulling away and brushing by Anne to* C) Who's going out? (*He puts his knife on the table, then crosses to the stove, lifts the lid and throws the star into the stove*)

ANNE. Why, of course. You're right. Of course we don't need them any more. (*She moves above the table, picks up Peter's knife and removes her star*)

(PETER *waits for her star to throw it away*)

I wonder what our friends will think when we don't show up today?

PETER. I didn't have any dates with anyone.

ANNE (*concentrating on her star*) Oh, I did. I had a date with Jopie this afternoon to go and play ping-pong at her house. Do you know Jopie de Waal?

PETER. No.

ANNE. Jopie's my best friend. I wonder what she'll think when she telephones and there's no answer? Probably she'll go over to the house—I wonder what she'll think—we left everything as if we'd suddenly been called away—breakfast dishes in the sink—beds not made . . . (*As she pulls off her star, the cloth underneath shows clearly the colour and form of the star*) Look! (*She puts the knife on the table*) It's still there.

(PETER *moves to* R *of Anne and looks at the mark, then picks up his knife and puts it in his pocket*)

What're you going to do with yours?

PETER. Burn it. (*He moves to the stove and holds out his hand for Anne's star*)

(ANNE *starts to give the star to Peter, but cannot and moves up* C, *above the table*)

ANNE. It's funny. I can't throw it away. I don't know why.

PETER (*with a step down; incredulously*) You can't throw . . .? Something they branded you with? That they made you wear so they could spit on you?

ANNE. I know. I know. But after all, it *is* the Star of David, isn't it?

(*The* VAN DAANS *have arranged their things, have put their clothes in the wardrobe and are sitting on the bed, fanning themselves. The chores are completed in the room* R.

Lighting Cue 6

MR FRANK *turns out the light in the room* R, *comes into the centre room and quietly closes the door*)

PETER. Maybe it's different for a girl.

(ANNE *puts her star in her school bag*)

MR FRANK (*crossing to* C) Forgive me, Peter. Now, let me see. We must find a bed for your cat.

(PETER *stands above the table.* ANNE *kneels and looks into Mouschi's case*)

I'm glad you brought your cat. Anne was feeling so badly about hers.

(ANNE *wanders below the table to* R, *inspecting everything, then kneels on the upstage end of the couch, giving it a thorough examination*)

(*He sees a small worn wash-tub and pulls it from the top shelf up* L)
Here we are. (*He gives the tub to Peter*) Will it be comfortable in
that?

PETER. Thanks.

MR FRANK (*indicating the room* L) And here is your room. But
I warn you, Peter, you can't grow any more. Not an inch, or
you'll have to sleep with your feet out of the skylight. (*He goes
to the door* L *and opens it*)

(PETER *crosses and puts the tub inside the door* L)

Are you hungry?

PETER (*gathering up his things from the chair and the floor*) No.

MR FRANK. We have some bread and butter.

PETER. No, thank you.

MR FRANK (*with a friendly pat on Peter's shoulder*) You can
have it for luncheon, then. And tonight we will have a real supper
—our first supper together.

PETER. Thanks. Thanks. (*He goes into the room* L)

(MR FRANK *closes the door after Peter, then sits* L *of the table and
removes his shoes*)

MR FRANK. That's a nice boy, Peter.

ANNE. He's awfully shy, isn't he?

MR FRANK. You'll like him, I know.

ANNE (*rising and crossing above the table to him*) I certainly hope
so, since he's the only boy I'm likely to see for months and
months.

MR FRANK. Anne, there's a box there. Will you open it?

(ANNE *goes over to the carton on the table* R *and transfers it to the
table* C.

Effects Cue 8

The sound of children playing is heard from the street below.
MR FRANK *goes to the sink and pours a glass of milk from the
thermos bottle*)

ANNE. You know the way I'm going to think of it here? I'm
going to think of it as a boarding-house. A very peculiar Summer
boarding-house, like the one that we . . . (*She breaks off as she looks
in the box*) Father! Father! My film stars. I was wondering where
they were—and Queen Wilhelmina. How wonderful!

MR FRANK (*moving to* L *of her*) There's something more. (*He
places the glass on the down* L *corner of the table*) Go on. Look further.

(ANNE *digs deeper into the box and brings out a velour-covered
book. She examines it in delighted silence for a moment, then opens the
cover slowly, and looks up at Mr Frank with shining eyes*)

ANNE. A diary! (*She throws her arms around him*) I've never had a diary. And I've always longed for one. (*She rushes to the table* R *and looks for a pencil*) Pencil, pencil, pencil, pencil. (*She darts across to the stair-well and starts down the stairs*) I'm going down to the office to get a pencil.

MR FRANK. Anne! No! (*He strides to Anne and catches her arm*)

(MRS FRANK, *aware of the sudden movement and sounds, sits up. After a moment she rises, goes to the window and looks out, then returns and sits on the bed*)

ANNE (*startled*) But there's no-one in the building now.

MR FRANK (*drawing her* C) It doesn't matter. I don't want you ever to go beyond that door.

ANNE (*sobered*) Never? Not even at night time, when everyone is gone? Or on Sundays? Can't I go down to listen to the radio?

MR FRANK. Never. I am sorry, Anneke. It isn't safe. No, you must never go beyond that door.

ANNE. I see. (*For the first time she realizes what "going into hiding" means*)

MR FRANK. It'll be hard, I know. But always remember this, Anneke. There are no walls, there are no bolts, no locks that anyone can put on your mind. Miep will bring us books. We will read history, poetry, mythology. (*He gives Anne the glass of milk*) Here's your milk.

(MR FRANK *puts his arm about* ANNE, *and crosses with her to the couch, where they sit side by side*)

As a matter of fact, between us, Anne, being here has certain advantages for you. For instance you remember the battle you had with your mother the other day on the subject of goloshes? You said you'd rather die than wear goloshes. But in the end you had to wear them. Well now, you see for as long as we are here you will never have to wear goloshes. Isn't that good? And the coat that you inherited from Margot——

(ANNE *makes a wry face*)

——you won't have to wear that. And the piano. You won't have to practise on the piano. I tell you, this is going to be a fine life for you.

(ANNE's *panic is gone.* PETER *appears in the doorway of his room, with a saucer in one hand and the cat in the other*)

PETER. I—I—I thought I'd better get some water for Mouschi before . . .

MR FRANK (*rising and moving to the sink*) Of course.

Effects Cue 9

(*The carillon begins its melody and strikes eight. As it does so,* MR FRANK *motions for Peter and Anne to be quiet, tiptoes to the window in the rear wall and peers down.* MR VAN DAAN *rises and moves to the head of the attic stairs.* MR FRANK *puts his finger to his lips, indicating to Anne and Peter that they must be silent, then steps down toward Peter indicating he can draw no water.* PETER *starts back to his room.* ANNE *rises and crosses below the table to Peter.* MR FRANK *crosses quietly towards the room* R. *As* PETER *reaches the door of his room a board creaks under his foot. The three are frozen for a minute in fear.* ANNE *then continues over to Peter on tiptoe and pours some milk in the saucer.* PETER *squats on the floor, putting the milk before the cat and encouraging him to drink.* MR FRANK *crosses to them, gives Anne his fountain pen, then crosses to the room* R, *goes inside, sits on the downstage bed and puts a comforting arm around Mrs Frank.* ANNE *squats for a moment beside Peter, watching the cat, then crosses to the chair* R *of the table, puts down the glass, sits on the chair with her feet tucked under her, opens her diary and writes. All are silent and motionless, except* MR VAN DAAN *who returns to Mrs Van Daan and fans her with a newspaper. The Westertoren finishes tolling the hour.*

Lighting Cue 7

As ANNE *begins to write, the* LIGHTS *fade except for a spotlight focused on Anne. Her voice is heard faintly at first, then with growing strength)*

ANNE. I expect I should be describing what it feels like to go into hiding.

Lighting Cue 8

(*The spotlight fades*)

But I really don't know yet, myself. I only know it's funny never to be able to go outdoors—never to breathe fresh air—never to run and shout and jump. It's the silence in the night that frightens me most. Every time I hear a creak in the house, or a step on the street outside, I'm sure they're coming for us. The days aren't so bad. At least we know that Miep and Mr Kraler are down there below us in the office. Our protectors, we call them. I asked father what would happen to them if the Nazis found out they were hiding us. Pim said that they would suffer the same fate that we would. Imagine! They know this and yet when they come up here, they're always cheerful and gay as if there were nothing in the world to bother them. Friday, the twenty-first of August, nineteen forty-two.

Lighting Cue 9

(*The* LIGHTS *come slowly up. Simultaneously* ANNE'S VOICE *begins to fade*)

Today I'm going to tell you our general news. Mother is unbearable. She insists on treating me like a baby, which I loathe. Otherwise things are going better. The weather is . . .

Scene 3

SCENE—*The same. August 1942. A few minutes after six p.m.*
   The furniture arrangement is as in the preceding scene except that an upright chair has been moved to above the table. A stack of books has appeared on Peter's window-seat. The dividing curtains are wide open and Anne's and Peter's shoes are on the floor in front of the table. Mrs Frank's knitting is on the table R. A bowl of green beans, yet to be sliced, is on the draining-board with a cooking pot alongside.

When the LIGHTS *come up the table-lamp* R *is lit. In the centre room,* MR FRANK, *with his shoes in his hand, is standing at the window up* C *looking down at the street below, waiting to see that the workmen have left the building. The group in the room watch him intently, waiting for his signal to be able to move.* MRS VAN DAAN *sits in the chair above the stair-well, her fur coat in her lap.* ANNE *and* PETER *are seated opposite each other at the table* C, *where they have been doing lessons in copybooks.* PETER *is* R *and* ANNE *is* L *of the table.* MRS FRANK *stands above the couch, shoes in hand, waiting to put them on.* MARGOT *is seated at the dressing-table in the room* R, *where she is studying.* MR VAN DAAN *is in the attic room, playing solitaire on the bed.*

Effects Cue 10

   From outside we hear the sounds of street traffic and the distant ships' sirens. After a couple of seconds of silence, MR FRANK *turns from the window.*

MR FRANK (*to the group; quietly*) It's safe now. The last workman has left.

   (*There is an immediate stir of relief and activity among the people in the main room*)

ANNE (*throwing her arms and legs wide in an exaggerated gesture of relief*) Whee! (*She rises*)
MRS FRANK (*startled and amused*) Anne!
MRS VAN DAAN (*rising*) I'm first for the W.C.

   (MRS VAN DAAN *hurries across and goes into the W.C., pausing only long enough to drape her coat carefully over the chair above the table* C.

Lighting Cue 10

   Inside the W.C. she turns on the light. MRS FRANK *puts on her shoes and goes to the sink to prepare supper. She puts on her apron and begins beating a bowl of batter.* ANNE *sneaks* PETER'S *shoes from under the table as he stretches, and hides them behind her back.* MR FRANK, *carrying his shoes, goes into the room* R)

MR FRANK (*to Margot*) Six o'clock. School's over. (*He sits on the downstage bed and puts on his shoes*)

(MARGOT *rises and stretches. In the centre room* ANNE *is watching as* PETER *tries to find his shoes. He remains seated as he peers under the table*)

PETER (*to Anne*)   Have you seen my shoes?

ANNE (*innocently*)   Your shoes?

PETER (*he knows*)   You've taken them, haven't you?

ANNE.   I don't know what you're talking about.

PETER (*half rising as he prepares to catch Anne*)   You're going to be sorry.

ANNE.   Am I? (*She holds the shoes tightly and makes a feint as if to run upstage*)

(PETER *lunges above the table to catch* ANNE, *who reverses and runs below the table to* MRS FRANK, *who is watching with amusement.* PETER *continues his circle of the table hot on Anne's heels, but is slowed as he becomes entangled in the chair* R *of the table which* ANNE *pulls into his path. She hides behind Mrs Frank but* PETER *manages to catch her hands. They struggle and fall to the floor up* L)

MRS FRANK (*protesting*)   Anne, dear!

PETER.   Wait till I get you.

ANNE.   I'm waiting.

(PETER *pins Anne down, wrestling to get the shoes*)

(*All through this action she has been having a wonderful time*) Don't! Don't! Peter, stop it. Ouch!

MRS FRANK.   Anne! Peter!

(PETER *suddenly becomes self-conscious, roughly grabs his shoes and moves towards the room* L)

ANNE (*catching Peter as he opens the door*)   Peter, where are you going? Come, dance with me.

PETER.   I tell you I don't know how.

ANNE.   I'll teach you.

PETER.   I'm going to give Mouschi his dinner.

ANNE.   Can I watch?

PETER.   He doesn't like people around while he eats.

ANNE.   Peter, please.

PETER.   No. (*He goes into the room* L)

(ANNE *slams the door after Peter*)

MRS FRANK.   Anne, dear, I think you shouldn't play like that with Peter. It's not dignified.

(ANNE *is now deflated and moves above the table* C, *inspecting her chafed elbows*)

ANNE.   Who cares if it's dignified? I don't want to be dignified. (*She throws herself across the chair* R *of the table in a most undignified manner*)

Lighting Cue 11

(Mr Frank *turns off the table-lamp* R. Margot *gives him her copybook. They come into the centre room.* Margot *moves to help Mrs Frank.* Mr Frank *moves below the table and gathers up Anne's copybooks.* Peter, *in the room* L, *puts on his shoes*)

Mrs Frank (*to Anne*)   You complain that I don't treat you like a grown-up. But when I do, you resent it.

(Margot *brings a cloth and wipes the table*)

Anne (*rising and replacing the chair* R *of the table*)   I only want some fun—someone to laugh and clown with. After you've sat still all day and hardly moved, you've got to have some fun. I don't know what's the matter with that boy.
Mr Frank. He isn't used to girls. Give him a little time.
Anne. Time? Isn't two months time? I could cry.

(Margot *moves towards the sink*)

(*She catches hold of Margot*) Come on, Margot—dance with me. Come on, please.
Margot (*pulling away*)   I have to help with supper. (*She returns to her duties with Mrs Frank*)
Anne. You know we're going to forget how to dance. When we get out we won't remember a thing. (*She sings to herself,* "*Ta-dum, Ta-dum, Ta-dum, Dum-dum*" *and waltzes down* L *of the table, then below it*)

(Mr Frank *is looking at Peter's copybook. As* Anne *approaches he holds out his arms and they do a few turns of a waltz, down* C.
Lighting Cue 12

Mrs Van Daan *turns off the W.C. light and comes into the room*)

Mrs Van Daan (*as she enters*)   Next? (*She looks around as she starts putting on her shoes*) Where's Peter?
Anne. Where would he be?

(Mr Frank *and* Anne *finish with a flourish and a bow.* Anne *continues singing quietly, circles* L *and up* LC. Mr Frank *sits* L *of the table and checks the copybooks*)

Mrs Van Daan. He hasn't finished his lessons, has he? His father'll kill him if he catches him in there with that cat and his work not done. (*She picks up her coat, crosses to the couch and sits*) Anne, get him out of there, will you?

(Anne *dances quickly to Peter's door and knocks in rhythm to her singing.* "*Ta-dum, Ta-dum, Ta-dum, Knock-knock.*")

Anne (*calling*)   Peter. Peter.
Peter (*opening the door a crack*)   What is it?
Anne. Your mother says to come out.

PETER. I'm giving Mouschi his dinner.

MRS VAN DAAN. You know what your father says. (*She arranges the coat carefully over her lap, caressing the fur and touching her cheek with the collar*)

PETER. For Heaven's sake, I haven't even looked at him since lunch.

MRS VAN DAAN. I'm just telling you, that's all.

ANNE. I'll feed him.

PETER. I don't want you in there.

MRS VAN DAAN. Peter!

PETER (*to Anne*) Then give him his dinner and come right out, you hear? (*He crosses to the chair R of the table and sits*)

(ANNE *goes into the room* L, *closes the door and disappears behind the curtain covering his closet*)

MRS VAN DAAN (*to Peter*) Now, is that any way to talk to your little girl friend?

PETER. Mother—for Heaven's sake—will you please stop saying that?

MRS VAN DAAN. Look at him blush. Look at him.

PETER (*uncomfortable*) Please. I'm not—anyway—let me alone, will you?

MRS VAN DAAN. He acts like it was something to be ashamed of. It's nothing to be ashamed of, to have a little girl friend.

PETER. You're crazy. She's only thirteen.

MRS VAN DAAN. So what? And you're sixteen. Just perfect. Your father's ten years older than I am. (*To Mr Frank*) I warn you, Mr Frank, if this war lasts much longer, you and I are going to be related.

MR FRANK. Mazeltov!

MRS FRANK (*moving to R of the table; deliberately*) I wonder where Miep is? She's usually so prompt.

Effects Cue 11

(*Suddenly everything else is forgotten as they listen to a sound in the street. It is the sound of an automobile coming to a sudden stop. The people in the room are tense, motionless in their terror. The car starts away. A wave of relief sweeps over the people.* MRS FRANK *returns to her dinner preparations.* MR FRANK *goes back to the copybooks.* ANNE *suddenly flings open the door of the room* L *and makes a dramatic entrance. She is dressed in Peter's "plus-fours", jacket and cap. She affects a long stride and a deep voice as she crosses below the table then circles to the chair above it.* PETER *looks at her in fury. The others are amused*)

ANNE. Good evening, everyone. Forgive me if I don't stay. I have a friend waiting for me in there. My friend Tom—Tom Cat. (*She hops on to the chair above the table and puts one foot on the table*)

Some people say that we look alike. But Tom has the most beautiful whiskers—— (*she strokes her imaginary whiskers*)

(PETER *rises and crosses above Anne towards the room* L)

—and I have only a little fuzz. I am hoping—in time . . .

PETER (*wheeling to* L *of Anne*) All right, Mrs Quack Quack.

ANNE (*jumping down and pushing Peter away; outraged*) Peter!

PETER. I heard about you—how you talked so much in class they called you "Mrs Quack Quack". (*He moves below the table and picks up his copybook*) How Mr Smitter made you write a composition—" 'Quack quack', said Mrs Quack Quack."

ANNE. Well, go on. Tell them the rest.

(ANNE *pursues* PETER *and gives him another shove as he picks up the book. She uses both hands and the trousers fall to her ankles. She hitches them up and continues after* PETER *as he crosses above the table to the door* L)

How it was so good he read it out loud to the class and then read it to all his other classes.

PETER. Quack! Quack! Quack-quack-quack.

ANNE (*pulling off the coat and trousers*) You are the most intolerable, insufferable boy I've ever met. (*She throws the clothes down the stair-well*)

(PETER *quickly places the book just inside the door of the room* L *and goes down the stair-well to collect the clothes.* MRS VAN DAAN *rises, leaves her coat on the couch and goes to the kitchen area to help with the supper preparations*)

MRS VAN DAAN. That's right, Anneke. Give it to him.

ANNE (*slumping in the chair above the stair-well*) With all the boys in the world—why I had to get locked up with one like you.

PETER (*coming up the stairs*) Quack, quack, quack, and from now on stay out of my room. (*He turns towards the room* L)

(ANNE *puts out her foot and trips* PETER, *who picks himself up, furious and inarticulate, and takes the clothes into his closet. The door is left open.* ANNE *is all innocence.* MRS FRANK *moves to* ANNE *and smoothes her hair. In doing so she feels* ANNE'S *forehead*)

MRS FRANK (*quietly*) Anne, dear—your hair. You're warm. Are you feeling all right?

ANNE (*rising and moving below the table*) Please, Mother. (*She slips her feet into her shoes*)

MRS FRANK. You haven't a fever, have you? (*She moves above the table to* R *of it*)

ANNE (*moving to the couch*) No. No.

MRS FRANK. Anneke, dear, don't do that. You know we can't call a doctor here, ever. There's only one thing to do—watch carefully. Prevent an illness before it comes. (*She moves to* L *of* ANNE)

(ANNE *turns her back*)

Let me see your tongue.
ANNE. Mother, this is perfectly absurd.
MRS FRANK. Anne, dear, don't be such a baby. Let me see your tongue.

(ANNE *shakes her head*)

(*She appeals to Mr Frank*) Otto . . .?
MR FRANK. You hear your mother, Anne.

(ANNE *turns her head towards her mother, sticks out her tongue for an instant, and immediately turns away*)

MRS FRANK (*good-naturedly*) Come on—open up.

(ANNE, *since she must, goes all the way and puts out her tongue as far as possible, and with her mouth wide open, leans towards her mother*)

You seem all right—but perhaps an aspirin . . . (*She returns to the sink*)

(ANNE *follows Mrs Frank to the sink.* MRS VAN DAAN *moves and stands above the table.* MR VAN DAAN, *in the attic, puts away his cards and comes down the stairs*)

MRS VAN DAAN. For Heaven's sake don't give that child any pills. I waited for fifteen minutes this morning for her to come out of the W.C.
ANNE. I was washing my hair.

(MRS VAN DAAN *crosses to the couch and sits*)

MR FRANK. I think there's nothing the matter with our Anne that a ride on her bike, or a visit with Jopie de Waal wouldn't cure. Isn't that so, Anne?

(ANNE *moves to Mr Frank and gives him a hug.* MR VAN DAAN *crosses to Mrs Van Daan.*

Effects Cue 12

The sound of a fleet of bombers is heard high overhead, along with bursts of ack-ack fire. This continues for some time)

MR VAN DAAN. Miep not come yet?
MRS VAN DAAN. The workmen just left, a little while ago.
MR VAN DAAN (*moving below the table*) What's for dinner tonight?
MRS VAN DAAN. Beans.
MR VAN DAAN (*stopping short and throwing a pained look back at his wife*) Not again!

Mrs Van Daan. Poor Putti! I know. But what can we do? That's all that Miep brought us.

(Mr Van Daan *resumes his pacing, moving* L. Anne *moves quickly behind him and follows him, imitating his posture and stride as he starts moving up towards the open door of the room* L)

Anne (*in a deep voice*) We are now in what is known as the "bean cycle". Beans boiled, beans en casserole, beans with strings, beans without strings . . .

(Mr Van Daan *sticks his head into the room* L *just as* Peter *starts out with his copybook*)

Mr Van Daan (*to Peter*) I saw you—in there, playing with your cat.

(Peter *crosses above the table to the chair* R *of it and sits.* Mrs Van Daan *spreads her coat across her lap and strokes the fur*)

Mrs Van Daan. He just went in for a second, putting his coat away. He's been out here all the time, doing his lessons.

Mr Frank (*looking up from the copybooks*) Anne, you got an excellent in your history paper today—and very good in Latin.

(Mr Van Daan *paces* R *in a pattern that will circle down* R, *across below the table, then up* L *again. His pacing reminds us of a caged animal*)

Anne (*sitting above the table*) How about algebra?

Mr Frank. I'll have to make a confession. Up until now I've managed to stay ahead of you in algebra. Today you caught up with me. We'll leave it to Margot to correct.

Anne. Isn't algebra *vile*, Pim?

Mr Frank. Vile!

Margot (*moving between Anne and Mr Frank*) How did I do?

Anne (*rising and patting Margot's head*) Excellent, excellent, excellent, excellent!

(Margot *brushes away Anne's hand.* Anne *crosses to* R)

Mr Frank (*to Margot*) You should have used the subjunctive here.

Margot. Should I? I thought—look here—I didn't use it here . . . (*She sits in the chair above the table*)

(Margot *and* Mr Frank *become absorbed in the copybooks*)

Anne (*moving to the sofa*) Mrs Van Daan, may I try on your coat?

Mrs Frank (*with a step towards Anne*) No, Anne.

(Mrs Van Daan *holds up the coat so that* Anne *can slip into it*)

Mrs Van Daan. It's all right—but be careful with it. My

father gave me that the year before he died. He always bought the best that money could buy.

ANNE. Mrs Van Daan, did you have a lot of boy friends before you were married?

MRS FRANK (*moving to Anne*) Anne, that's a personal question. It's not courteous to ask personal questions.

MRS VAN DAAN. Oh, I don't mind.

(MRS FRANK *returns to her duties*)

(*To Anne*) Our house was always swarming with boys. When I was a girl we had . . .

MR VAN DAAN (*moving above the right end of the table*) Oh, God! Not again.

MRS VAN DAAN (*good-humouredly*) Shut up! (*She continues without a pause to Anne*)

(MR VAN DAAN *mimics Mrs Van Daan, speaking the first few words in unison with her, as he paces down* R, *then crosses below the table to* L *and goes up* L)

One Summer we had a big house in Hilversum. The boys came buzzing around like bees around a jam pot. And when I was sixteen—we were wearing our skirts very short those days and I had good-looking legs. (*She rises, crosses and stands below Mr Frank. She is very flirtatious*) I still have 'em. I may not be as pretty as I used to be, but I still have my legs. (*She pulls up her skirt to above her knees*)

(MR FRANK *is a bit nonplussed as he looks up and sees Mrs Van Daan*)

How about it, Mr Frank?

MR VAN DAAN (*moving above the table*) All right. All right. We see them.

MRS VAN DAAN. I'm not asking you. I'm asking Mr Frank.

PETER. Mother, for Heaven's sake . . .!

MRS VAN DAAN. Oh, I embarrass you, do I? (*She crosses to Anne, giving Peter a pat as she passes*) Well, I just hope the girl you marry has as good. (*To Anne*) My father used to worry about me, with so many boys hanging round. He told me, if any of them gets fresh, you say to him (*she places one hand on Anne's shoulder and with the other holds up a warning finger*)——

(MR VAN DAAN *moves down* L *and listens*)

—"Remember, Mr So-and-So, remember I'm a lady." (*She gives Anne a little tap on the cheek*)

ANNE (*imitating the action and delivery of Mrs Van Daan*) "Remember, Mr So-and-So, remember I'm a lady."

(MRS VAN DAAN *takes the coat from* ANNE, *who moves down* C *and sprawls on her stomach on the floor with her head* L *and her feet* R.

Her legs are spread wide as she listens for sounds below with an ear pressed to the boards)

Mr Van Daan (*to his wife*) Look at you, talking that way in front of her. Don't you know she puts it all down in that diary?
Mrs Van Daan. So if she does? I'm only telling the truth. (*She sits on the couch*)

(Mrs Frank *collects a tablecloth from the shelves* L *and moves above the table.* Margot *takes all the books from Mr Frank, crosses and puts them on the mantelpiece, then goes to the shelves up* L *and collects seven plates*)

Mrs Frank. Would you mind, Peter, if I moved you over to the couch?
Anne (*listening*) Miep must have the radio on.

(Mr Van Daan *crosses above the table to the couch.* Peter *rises and turns towards the couch*)

Mr Van Daan (*confronting Peter*) Haven't you finished yet?
Peter. No.
Mr Van Daan. You ought to be ashamed of yourself. (*He paces below the table* L *and is irritated when he has to step over one of Anne's widespread legs*)

Effects Cue 12a

(*The sound of the aircraft and ack-ack fades*)

Peter. All right. All right. I'm a dunce. I'm a hopeless case. Why do I go on? (*He sits above Mrs Van Daan on the couch*)

(Mrs Frank *spreads the tablecloth.* Margot *brings the plates and puts them on the table, then goes to the shelves up* L *and collects knives and forks*)

Mrs Van Daan (*to Peter*) You're not hopeless. Don't talk that way. It's just that you haven't anyone to help you, like the girls have. (*To Mr Frank*) Maybe you could help him, Mr Frank?

(Mr Van Daan *continues his circular path around the table and stands above the right end of it*)

Mr Frank. I'm sure that his father . . .
Mr Van Daan. Not me. I can't do anything with him. He won't listen to me. You go ahead—if you want.
Mr Frank (*rising and crossing below the table*) What about it, Peter? (*He steps over Anne's upstage leg*) Shall we make our school co-educational?

(Mr Van Daan *strides across Anne's lower leg as he moves* L)

Mrs Van Daan (*rising and crossing below Mr Frank to* L *of him*) You're an angel, Mr Frank.

(MARGOT *sets out the knives and forks on the table*)

An angel! (*She takes Mr Frank's face in her hands and kisses him on his mouth*) I don't know why I didn't meet you before I met— (*she indicates Mr Van Daan*) that one there. Here, sit down, Mr Frank.

(PETER *moves along the seat to the downstage end as* MRS VAN DAAN *pushes* MR FRANK *down on the couch*)

(*She sits at the upstage end of the couch with her arm over Mr Frank's shoulder*) Now, Peter, you listen to Mr Frank.

MR FRANK (*uncomfortable*) It might be better for us to go into Peter's room.

(MRS FRANK *watches all this as she works above the table.* PETER *jumps up eagerly and leads towards the room* L)

MRS VAN DAAN. That's right. You go in there, Peter. You listen to Mr Frank. Mr Frank is a highly educated man.

(MR FRANK *rises and follows close on Peter's heels.* MRS FRANK *intercepts him as he reaches the door* L *and wipes the lipstick from his lips.* PETER *goes into the room* L. MR FRANK, *embarrassed, hurries in after Peter. During the following scene he and* PETER *sit on the bed and* MR FRANK *helps Peter with his lessons.* MR VAN DAAN, *meanwhile, circles the table and crosses below it to* L, *again stepping over Anne*)

ANNE (*listening*) Shh! I can hear a man's voice talking.

MR VAN DAAN (*to Anne*) Isn't it bad enough here without your sprawling all over the place?

(ANNE *scrambles to a sitting position, with her back against the table*)

MRS VAN DAAN (*to her husband*) If you didn't smoke so much, you wouldn't be so bad-tempered.

MR VAN DAAN. Am I smoking? Do you see me smoking?

(MRS VAN DAAN *rises and paces up and down* RC *as the words get hotter*)

MRS VAN DAAN. Don't tell me you've used up all those cigarettes?

MR VAN DAAN. One package! Miep only brought me one package.

MRS VAN DAAN (*overlapping*) It's a filthy habit, anyway. It's a good time to break yourself.

MR VAN DAAN (*more heatedly*) Oh, stop it, please!

MRS VAN DAAN (*shouting*) You're smoking up all our money. You know that, don't you?

(MRS FRANK *and* MARGOT *studiously keep their eyes down, but* ANNE, *seated on the floor, follows the discussion interestedly*)

MR VAN DAAN (*shouting her down*) Will you shut up? (*He turns to see Anne staring up at him*) And what are you staring at?

ANNE. I never heard grown-ups quarrel before. I thought only children quarrelled.

MR VAN DAAN. This isn't a quarrel. It's a discussion. (*He turns away, then back for a final shot*) And I never heard children so rude before. (*He moves down* L)

ANNE (*rising; indignantly*) I—rude? (*She pursues Mr Van Daan* L)

(MARGOT *collects spoons from the shelves up* L *and places them around the table*)

MRS FRANK (*sitting above the table; quickly*) Anne, will you bring me my knitting?

(ANNE *crosses to the table* R *and picks up the knitting*)

I must remember, when Miep comes, to ask her to bring me some more wool.

MARGOT (*crossing to the room* R) I need some hairpins and some soap. I made a list. (*She goes into the room* R)

Lighting Cue 13

(MARGOT *turns on the table-lamp and writes out her list at the dressing-table*)

MRS FRANK (*to Anne*) Have you some library books for Miep when she comes?

(MR VAN DAAN *moves up* C. MRS VAN DAAN *sits on the downstage end of the couch*)

ANNE (*moving and handing the knitting to Mrs Frank*) It's ·a wonder that Miep has a life of her own the way we make her run errands for us. "Please, Miep, get me some starch." (*She addresses Mr Van Daan*) "Please take my hair out and have it cut." "Tell me all the latest news, Miep." (*She kneels above Mrs Van Daan on the couch*) Did you know she was engaged? His name is Dirk and Miep's afraid the Nazis will ship him off to Germany to work in one of their war plants. That's what they're doing with some of the young Dutchmen—they pick them up off the streets . . .

MR VAN DAAN (*crossing to* L *of Anne; irritated*) Don't you ever get tired of talking? Suppose you try keeping still for five minutes. Just five minutes. (*He slaps the back of one hand into the palm of the other to emphasize his point and paces to* L *in another swing around the table*)

(ANNE *clamps her lips tight, rises, and strides behind Mr Van Daan, mimicking him. As she passes* MRS FRANK, *she jumps up, takes Anne by the arm and detours her to the sink*)

MRS FRANK. Come here, Anne. Finish your glass of milk (*She gives a glass of milk to Anne, then sits above the table and knits*)

B

(MR VAN DAAN *walks rapidly down around the table again, ending up* L *and looking over the shelves*)

MR VAN DAAN (*as he moves*)   Talk, talk, talk. I never heard such a child. Where is my . . .? Every evening it's the same, talk, talk, talk. (*He looks around*) Where the . . .?

MRS VAN DAAN. What're you looking for?

MR VAN DAAN (*moving* C)   My pipe. Have you seen my pipe?

MRS VAN DAAN. What good's a pipe? You haven't got any tobacco.

MR VAN DAAN (*crossing to the room* R)   At least I'll have some-thing to hold in my mouth. (*He opens the door* R *and sticks his head in*) Margot, have you seen my pipe?

(ANNE, *behind Mr Van Daan's back, steals to the table* R, *places the glass of milk on it and snatches up his pipe. She then retreats up* RC *with lips still clamped and hiding the pipe behind her back*)

MARGOT. It was on the table last night.

MR VAN DAAN. I know. I know. (*He slams the door shut and turns to look on the mantelpiece*) Anne, did you see my pipe?

(ANNE *does not reply*)

(*He turns slowly to her*) Anne!

MRS FRANK. Anne, dear, Mr Van Daan is speaking to you.

ANNE (*feigning surprise; through tight lips*)   Am I allowed to talk now?

MR VAN DAAN. You're the most aggravating . . . (*He controls himself with difficulty*) The trouble with you is, you've been spoiled. What you need is a good old-fashioned spanking.

ANNE (*mimicking Mrs Van Daan*)   "Remember, Mr So-and-So, remember I'm a lady." (*She thrusts the pipe into Mr Van Daan's mouth, then picks up her glass of milk, crosses and stands down* LC)

(MARGOT *comes out of the room* R *with the list, places it on the table* R, *then moves to the kitchen area*)

MR VAN DAAN. Why aren't you nice and quiet like your sister Margot? Why do you have to show off all the time?

(ANNE *darts* R, *trying to get around* MR VAN DAAN, *but he retreats, blocking her way. He ends* R *of the table.* ANNE *is below and slightly* L *of Mr Van Daan, facing upstage*)

Let me give you a little advice, young lady. Men don't like that kind of thing in a girl. You know that? A man likes a girl who'll listen to him once in a while—a domestic girl, who'll keep her house shining for her husband—who loves to cook and sew and . . .

ANNE. I'd cut my throat first. I'd open my veins.

(MR VAN DAAN *moves up* L)

I'm going to be remarkable. I'm going to Paris.

Mr Van Daan (*derisively*) Paris!

Anne. To study music and art.

Mr Van Daan. Yeah—yeah.

Anne. I'm going to be a famous dancer or singer—or something wonderful. (*Arms held wide, milk in her right hand, she makes a dancer's turn. The milk spills over the fur coat on Mrs Van Daan's lap*)

(Mrs Van Daan *is shocked and stunned.* Anne *falls to her knees and tries to brush the milk away.* Margot *hurries down to them with a tea towel*)

Mrs Van Daan (*scarcely able to speak*) Now look what you've done—you clumsy little fool. My beautiful fur coat my father gave me.

Anne. I'm so sorry.

Mrs Van Daan. What do you care? It isn't yours—so go on, ruin it. Do you know what that coat cost? Do you? And now look at it. Look at it.

Anne. I'm very, very sorry.

Mrs Van Daan (*rising and crossing below the table to the attic stairs*) I could kill you for this. I could just kill you. (*She goes up the stairs, clutching her coat*)

Mr Van Daan (*following his wife*) Petronella—liefje—come back—the supper—come back. (*He goes up into the attic*)

Lighting Cue 14

(Mr Van Daan *switches on the attic light*)

Mrs Frank. Anne, you mustn't behave in that way.

(Margot *returns to the sink, taking the glass and cloth with her*)

Anne (*still kneeling*) It was an accident. Anyone can have an accident.

Mrs Frank. I don't mean that. I mean the answering back. You must not answer back.

(Anne *rises and crosses above the table to* l. *She walks heel-to-toe along a crack in the floor and continues down* l)

They are our guests. We must always show the greatest courtesy to them. We're all living under terrible tension. That's why we must control ourselves. You don't hear Margot getting into arguments with them, do you? Watch Margot. She's always courteous with them. Never familiar. She keeps her distance. And they respect her for it. Try to be like Margot.

Anne (*turning and moving up* l) And have them walk all over me, the way they do her? No, thanks.

Mrs Frank. I'm not afraid that anyone is going to walk all over you, Anne. I'm afraid for other people, that you'll walk on them. I don't know what happens to you, Anne. You are wild, self-willed. If I had ever talked to my mother as you talk to me . . .

ANNE. Things have changed. People aren't like that any more. "Yes, Mother." "No, Mother." "Anything you say, Mother." I've got to fight things out for myself. Make something of myself. (*She turns away*)

MRS FRANK. It isn't necessary to fight to do it. Margot doesn't fight, and isn't she . . .?

ANNE (*wheeling on her mother; violently rebellious*) Margot! Margot! Margot! Margot! That's all I hear from everyone— how wonderful Margot is—"Why aren't you like Margot?"

MARGOT (*moving up* C; *protesting*) Oh, come on, Anne, don't be so . . .

ANNE (*paying no attention*) Everything she does is right, and everything I do is wrong. I'm the goat around here. You're all against me—and you worst of all. (*She rushes off into the room* R *and throws herself down on the chaise-longue, stifling her sobs*)

(MRS FRANK *sighs, rises, crosses and puts her knitting on the mantelpiece*)

MRS FRANK. Let's put the soup on the stove—if there's anyone who cares to eat. Margot, will you take the bread out?

(MARGOT *takes the bread from the sink cupboard*)

(*Her agitation carries her* L) I don't know how we can go on living this way—I can't say a word to Anne—she flies at me.

MARGOT (*crossing to the shelves up* L) You know Anne. (*She takes a bread plate from the shelves*) In half an hour she'll be out here, laughing and joking.

MRS FRANK (*pacing to* C, *then down* R) And—(*she makes a motion upwards, indicating the Van Daans*) I told your father it wouldn't work—but no—no—he had to ask them, he said—he owed it to him, he said. Well, he knows now that I was right. These quarrels—this bickering . . .

MARGOT (*placing the bread on the table; with a warning look*) Shush! Shush!

Effects Cue 13

(*The buzzer for the door sounds. The buzzer signal used by Miep and Kraler is always the International Code "V". Dit-dit-dit-dah.* MRS FRANK, *startled, gasps*)

MRS FRANK. Every time I hear that sound my heart stops.
MARGOT (*crossing to the door* L) It's Miep. (*She knocks at the door*) Father.

Lighting Cue 15

(*The attic light is switched off.* MR FRANK *rises, comes quickly from the room* L *and hurries down the stair-well*)

Mr Frank (*as he goes*)   Thank you, Margot. Has everyone his list?

Margot.   I'll get my books. (*She indicates to Mrs Frank the list on the table* R) Here's your list. (*She goes into the room* R)

(Mrs Frank *goes to the table* R *and collects the list.* Anne *sits up, hiding her tears*)

(*To Anne*) Miep's here. (*She picks up her books and returns to the centre room*)

(Anne *rises, looks in the mirror and smooths her hair.* Mr Van Daan *comes down from the attic*)

Mr Van Daan.   Is it Miep?

Margot.   Yes. Father's gone down to let her in.

Mr Van Daan (*moving above the table*)   At last I'll have some cigarettes.

Mrs Frank (*moving to* L *of Mr Van Daan*)   I can't tell you how unhappy I am about Mrs Van Daan's coat. Anne should never have touched it.

Mr Van Daan.   She'll be all right.

Mrs Frank.   Is there anything I can do?

Mr Van Daan.   Don't worry. (*He turns towards the stair-well*)

(Kraler *and* Mr Frank *come up the stair-well. Their faces are grave.* Anne *and* Peter *come from their rooms.* Mrs Frank *moves below the table and meets* Kraler C)

Mrs Frank.   Mr Kraler!

Effects Cue 14

(*The sound of a streetcar is heard*)

Mr Van Daan (*shaking Kraler's hand across the table*)   How are you, Mr Kraler?

Margot.   This is a surprise.

Mrs Frank.   When Mr Kraler comes the sun begins to shine.

Mr Van Daan.   Miep is coming?

Kraler.   Not tonight.

(Mr Van Daan *moves up* C *in disgust.* Margot *puts her books on the right end of the table*)

Mrs Frank (*to Kraler*)   Wouldn't you like a cup of coffee— or, better still, will you have supper with us?

Kraler.   No, thank you.

Mr Frank (*moving down* L)   Mr Kraler has something to talk over with us. Something has happened, he says, which demands an immediate decision.

Mrs Frank (*fearfully*)   What is it?

(Kraler *crosses to the couch, sits, opens his briefcase and takes out a quart bottle of milk, two cabbages and a loaf of bread. He gives*

the food to MARGOT *and* ANNE, *who put it in the sink cupboard.*
MRS FRANK *sits* R *of the table.* PETER *stands* L *of the table.* MR
VAN DAAN *sits above the table*)

KRALER. Usually, when I come up here, I try to bring you
some bit of good news. What's the use of telling you the bad news
when there's nothing that you can do about it? But today something has happened. Dirk—Miep's Dirk, you know, came to me
just now. He tells me that he has a Jewish friend living near him.
A dentist. He says he's in trouble. He begged me, could I do
anything for this man—could I find him a hiding place? So I've
come to you. I know it's a terrible thing to ask of you, living as
you are, but would you take him in with you?

MR FRANK (*moving* C) Of course we will.

KRALER (*rising and crossing to* R *of Mr Frank*) It'll be just for
a night or two—until I find some other place. This happened
so suddenly that I didn't know where to turn.

MR FRANK. Where is he?

KRALER. Downstairs in the office.

MR FRANK. Good. Bring him up.

KRALER (*crossing to the stair-well*) His name is Dussel—Jan
Dussel.

MR FRANK (*moving to Kraler*) Dussel—I think I know him.

KRALER. I'll get him.

(KRALER *exits quickly down the stair-well.* MR FRANK *suddenly
becomes conscious of the others*)

MR FRANK. Forgive me. I spoke without consulting you. But
I knew you'd feel as I do.

MR VAN DAAN. There's no reason for you to consult anyone.
(*He rises and moves down* R) This is your place. You have a right
to do exactly as you please. The only thing I feel—there's so
little food as it is—and to take in another person . . .

(PETER, *ashamed of his father, turns away up* L)

MR FRANK. We can stretch the food a little. It's only for a
few days.

MR VAN DAAN (*sitting on the couch*) You want to make a bet?

MRS FRANK. I think it's fine to have him. But, Otto, where
are you going to put him? Where?

PETER (*moving above the left end of the table*) He can have my
bed. I can sleep on the floor. I wouldn't mind.

MR FRANK (*moving to* L *of Peter*) That's good of you, Peter.
But your room's too small, even for *you.*

Effects Cue 15

(*The sound of marching feet is heard off.* PETER *moves to the
window up* C *and looks out*)

ANNE. I have a much better idea. I'll come in here with you

and mother, and Margot can take Peter's room and Peter can
go in our room with Mr Dussel.

Margot (*moving above the right end of the table*) That's right.
We could do that.

Mr Frank. No, Margot. You mustn't sleep in that room—
neither you nor Anne. Mouschi has caught some rats in there.
Peter's brave. He doesn't mind.

Anne (*insistently*) Then how about *this*? I'll come in here with
you and mother and Mr Dussel can have my bed.

Mrs Frank. No. Margot will come in here with us and he
can have her bed. It's the only way. Margot, bring your things
in here. Help her, Anne.

(Margot *hurries into the room* R *to collect her things.* Peter
moves to the door R *to assist Margot*)

Anne (*to Mrs Frank; rebelliously*) Why Margot? Why can't I
come in here?

Mrs Frank. Because it wouldn't be proper for Margot to
sleep with a . . . Please, Anne. Don't argue. Please.

(Anne *moves indignantly to the door* R)

Mr Frank (*to Anne*) You don't mind sharing your room with
Mr Dussel, do you, Anne?

Anne (*hiding her hurt*) No. No, of course not.

Mr Frank. Good.

(Margot *hands her bath-robe to* Peter *who hangs it above the
shelves up* L. Anne *goes into the room* R, *collects Margot's nightgown
and hangs it on the shelves up* L. Margot *brings out a skirt and a
blouse, hangs them up, then returns for a small box with her comb,
brush, jewellery, etc. which she places on the shelves.* Mrs Van Daan,
having composed herself, comes down from the attic)

Where's the cognac?

Mrs Frank (*indicating the shelves up* L) It's there. But, Otto,
I was saving it in case of illness.

Mr Frank. I think we couldn't find a better time to use it.
Peter, will you get five glasses for me? (*He collects the bottle from
the shelves*)

(Peter *collects five glasses from the shelf over the sink, puts them
on the table then moves to the door of the room* L. Mr Frank *gives the
bottle to* Mrs Frank *who pours a swallow into each glass*)

Mrs Van Daan (*crossing to the couch*) What's happening?
What's going on?

Mr Van Daan (*sourly*) Someone's moving in with us.

Mrs Van Daan (*sitting below her husband on the couch*) In here?
You're joking.

MARGOT. It's only for a night or two—until Mr Kraler finds him another place.

MR VAN DAAN. Yeah! Yeah!

(KRALER *comes up the stair-well.*

MR DUSSEL *follows him up. He is a man in his fifties, meticulous and finicky, but at the moment, bewildered. He carries a brief-case and a shopping bag, stuffed full, and has a small medicine case tucked under his arm. He wears a raincoat and hat.* MR FRANK *hurries to the stair-well and holds out his hand.* ANNE, *all eyes, sits above the table*)

MR FRANK. Come in, Mr Dussel.

KRALER. This is Mr Frank.

DUSSEL. Mr Otto Frank?

MR FRANK. Yes. Let me take your things.

(MR FRANK *takes the hat and bags and hands them to* PETER, *who puts them under the shelves up* L. DUSSEL *clings to his medicine case*)

This is my wife, Edith—and Mrs Van Daan, and Mr Van Daan —their son, Peter—and my daughters, Margot and Anne.

(DUSSEL *shakes hands with everyone, crossing to the Van Daans*)

KRALER. Thank you, Mr Frank. Thank you all. Mr Dussel, I leave you in good hands. Oh—Dirk's coat . . . (*He moves down* L)

(DUSSEL *crosses hurriedly to Kraler and takes off his coat. Underneath is his white office jacket, with a yellow Star of David on it*)

DUSSEL (*to Kraler*) What can I say to thank you? (*He hands the coat to Kraler*)

MRS FRANK (*rising and handing drinks to the Van Daans; to Dussel*) Mr Kraler and Miep—they're our life-line. Without them we couldn't live.

(DUSSEL *sinks on to the chair* L *of the table*)

KRALER. Please. Please. You make us seem very heroic. It isn't that at all.

(MRS FRANK *offers a drink to* KRALER, *who refuses it, so she places it before Dussel.* MR FRANK *moves and stands above Dussel.* MARGOT *goes into the room* R, *straightens the beds and sees that all is orderly*)

(*He moves to* L *of Mr Frank*) We simply don't like the Nazis. We don't like their methods. We don't like anything about them.

MR FRANK (*smiling*) I know. I know. "No-one's going to tell us Dutchmen what to do with our damn Jews."

KRALER (*to Dussel*) Pay no attention to Mr Frank. I'll be up

tomorrow to see that they're treating you right. (*To Mr Frank*)
Don't trouble to come down again. Peter will bolt the door after
me, won't you, Peter?

PETER (*moving quickly*) Yes, sir.

MR FRANK. Thank you, Peter. I'll do it.

KRALER. Good night. Good night.

ALL (*ad lib.*) Good night, Mr Kraler. See you tomorrow, etc.
etc.

> (DUSSEL *rises.*
> KRALER *and* MR FRANK *exit down the stair-well*)

MRS FRANK. Please, Mr Dussel, sit down. (*She sits* R *of the
table*)

> (DUSSEL *resumes his seat* L *of the table.* PETER *moves down* L
> *and sits on the floor, facing Dussel*)

DUSSEL. I'm dreaming. I know it. I can't believe my eyes.
Mr Otto Frank, here. (*To Mrs Frank*) You're not in Switzerland,
then? A woman told me . . . She said she'd gone to your house—
the door was open, everything was in disorder, dishes in the sink.
She said she found a piece of paper in the waste basket with an
address scribbled on it—an address in Zurich. She said you must
have escaped to Zurich.

> (MARGOT *brings her slippers out of the room* R, *puts them up* L,
> *then returns for a final check of the room*)

ANNE. Father put that there purposely—just so people would
think that very thing.

DUSSEL. And you've been *here* all this time?

MRS FRANK. All this time—ever since July.

> (MARGOT *comes into the centre room and stands above the table,*
> R *of Anne.*
> MR FRANK *enters up the stair-well*)

ANNE (*to Mr Frank*) It worked, Pim—the address you left.
Mr Dussel says that people believe we escaped to Switzerland.

MR FRANK (*standing above the left end of the table*) I'm glad.
Let's have a little drink to welcome Mr Dussel. (*He lifts his glass
and begins his welcoming toast*)

> (*All the grown-ups, except* DUSSEL, *rise.* MR FRANK *breaks off as*
> DUSSEL *bolts his drink. All are amused*)

(*He begins again*) To Mr Dussel. Welcome. We're very honoured
to have you with us.

MRS FRANK. To Mr Dussel, welcome.

> (*The* VAN DAANS *murmur a welcome. The grown-ups drink.*
> DUSSEL *is embarrassed as he realizes he has bolted his drink ahead
> of time.* ANNE *pantomimes drinking a big drink*)

MRS VAN DAAN. Um. That was good. (*She sits on the sofa*)

(MRS FRANK *gives Margot a sip of her drink, but* MARGOT *does not like it*)

MR VAN DAAN (*to Dussel*) Did Mr Kraler warn you that you won't get much to eat here? You can imagine—three ration books among the seven of us—and now you make *eight*.

Effects Cue 16

(*The sound of the street organ is heard.* MRS VAN DAAN *tugs at her husband's coat-tail.* PETER, *humiliated, rises and moves up* L)

DUSSEL. Mr Van Daan, you don't realize what is happening outside that you should warn me of a thing like that. You don't realize what's going on.

(MR VAN DAAN *puts his glass on the table* R *and resumes his characteristic pacing upstage*)

(*He continues to the others*) Right here in Amsterdam every day hundreds of Jews disappear. They surround a block and search house by house. Children come back from school to find their parents gone. Hundreds are being deported—people that you and I know—the Hallensteins—the Wessels . . .

MRS FRANK (*sitting* R *of the table; in tears*) Oh, no. No!

DUSSEL (*rising and moving below the table*) They get their call-up notice—come to the Jewish theatre on such and such a day and hour—bring only what you can carry in a rucksack. (*He crosses to the couch*) And if you refuse the call-up notice, then they come and drag you from your home and ship you off to Mauthausen. The death camp.

MRS FRANK. We didn't know that things had got so much worse.

DUSSEL (*sitting above Mrs Van Daan on the couch*) Forgive me for speaking so.

ANNE (*rising and crossing to Dussel*) Do you know the De Waals? Do you know what has become of them? Their daughter Jopie and I were in the same class. Jopie's my best friend.

DUSSEL. They are gone.

ANNE. Gone?

DUSSEL. With all the others.

ANNE. Oh, no. Not Jopie! (*She moves up* R, *in tears*)

(MARGOT *puts her arm comfortingly around Anne*)

MRS VAN DAAN. There were some people called Wagner. They lived near us . . .

MR FRANK (*with a glance at Anne; interrupting*) I think we should put this off until later. (*He moves below the table*) We all have many questions we want to ask—but I'm sure that Mr Dussel would like to get settled before supper.

(PETER *gets Dussel's things and hands them across the table to* MR FRANK)

DUSSEL (*rising and crossing to* C)   Thank you. I would. I brought very little with me.

MR FRANK (*handing the hat and bags to Dussel*) I'm sorry we can't give you a room alone. But I hope you won't be too uncomfortable. We've had to make strict rules here—a schedule of hours. We'll tell you after supper. Anne, would you like to take Mr Dussel to his room? (*He moves around the left end of the table, then crosses to Anne*)

(DUSSEL *takes a few steps after Mr Frank then turns back*)

ANNE (*controlling her tears*)   If you'll come with me, Mr Dussel. (*She moves to the door of the room* R)

DUSSEL (*crossing to Mrs Van Daan and shaking her hand*)   Forgive me if I haven't really expressed my gratitude to all of you. (*He shakes hands with Mrs Frank, then crosses slowly below the table and moves up* L *to Peter*) This has been such a shock to me. (*He shakes hands with Peter*) I'd always thought of myself as Dutch. I was born in Holland. My father was born in Holland, and my grandfather. (*He moves to Margot and shakes hands with her*) And now—after all these years . . . (*He breaks off*) If you'll excuse me. (*He shakes hands with Mr Van Daan, then with Mr Frank and follows Anne into the room* R)

Lighting Cue 16

(ANNE *switches on the pendant in the room* R)

ANNE. Well, here we are. (*She closes the door*)

(DUSSEL *looks around the room. In the centre room* MR FRANK *places a comforting hand on his wife's shoulder.* MARGOT *picks up the cognac*)

MARGOT. The news sounds pretty bad, doesn't it? It's so different from what Mr Kraler tells us. Mr Kraler says things are improving.

MR VAN DAAN. I like it better the way Kraler tells it.

(MARGOT, *during the following scene, returns the cognac to the shelf up* L, *then collects the glasses, takes them to the sink, rinses and dries them.* MRS VAN DAAN *rises and goes with* MR VAN DAAN *up to the attic.* PETER *goes into the room* L. MR FRANK *sits in the chair above the stair-well.* MRS FRANK *rises, goes to the kitchen area, gets a bread basket, crosses and hands it to* MR FRANK, *who rises, crosses and goes behind the curtain up* R. MRS FRANK *then gets an iron from the shelves up* L *and follows Mr Frank off. In the room* R, ANNE, L *of* DUSSEL, *turns to him*)

ANNE. You're going to share the room with me.

DUSSEL. I'm a man who's always lived alone. I haven't had

to adjust myself to others. I hope you'll bear with me until I learn.

ANNE. Let me help you. (*She takes the bags and places them on the cot* R) Do you always live all alone? Have you no family at all?

DUSSEL. No-one. (*He opens his medicine case and spreads the bottles on the dressing-table*)

ANNE. How dreadful! You must be terribly lonely.

DUSSEL. I'm used to it.

(PETER, *in the room* L, *takes the cat from the case and holds it up so it can look out of the skylight*)

ANNE. I don't think I could ever get used to it. Didn't you even have a pet? A cat, or a dog?

DUSSEL. I have an allergy for fur-bearing animals. They give me asthma.

ANNE. Oh, dear! Peter has a cat.

DUSSEL. Here? (*The very thought makes him choke up*) He has it here?

ANNE. Yes. But we hardly ever see it. He keeps it in his room all the time. I'm sure it will be all right.

DUSSEL. Let us hope so. (*He hastily sips some medicine from one of his bottles*)

ANNE. That's Margot's bed, where you're going to sleep. I sleep on the sofa there. (*She indicates the empty hooks*) We cleared these off for your things (*She climbs up on the window-seat and peers out*)

(DUSSEL *sits on the cot* R *to test its softness and is disappointed with it. As Anne continues, he tests her sofa and finds it more comfortable*)

The best part about this room—you can look down and see a bit of the street and the canal. There's a houseboat—you can see the end of it—a bargeman lives there with his family. They have a baby and he's just beginning to walk and I'm so afraid he's going to fall into the canal some day. I watch him . . .

DUSSEL (*moving to Anne; interrupting*) Your father spoke of a schedule.

ANNE. Oh, yes. (*She steps down, then urges him to climb up for a look*)

(DUSSEL *steps on to the window-seat and peers out of the window*)

It's mostly about the times we have to be quiet. And times for the W.C. (*Without any false shame*) You can use it now, if you like.

DUSSEL (*stepping down and crossing to the dressing-table; stiffly*) No, thank you.

ANNE. I suppose you think it's awful, my talking about a thing like that. But you don't know how important it can get to be, especially when you're frightened.

(DUSSEL *looks at Anne, appalled at the turn their conversation has taken. As she continues, he takes off his jacket and places it with his bags*)

About this room, the way Margot and I did—she had it to herself in the afternoons for studying, reading—lessons, you know—and I took the mornings. Would that be all right with you?

DUSSEL (*removing his tie*) I'm not at my best in the morning.

ANNE. You stay here in the morning, then. I'll take the room in the afternoon.

DUSSEL. Tell me, when you're in here, what happens to me? Where am I spending my time? In there, with all the people?

ANNE. Yes.

DUSSEL. I see, I see.

ANNE. We have supper at half-past six.

DUSSEL (*moving to the downstage bed and lying on it, facing front*) Then, if you don't mind—I like to lie down quietly for ten minutes before eating. I find it helps the digestion.

ANNE. Of course. (*She wonders if she should tell Dussel he is on the wrong bed, decides not to, moves to him and bends over him*) I hope I'm not going to be too much of a bother to you. I seem to be able to get everyone's back up.

DUSSEL (*complacently*) I always get along very well with children. My patients all bring their children to me, because they know I get on well with them. So don't you worry about that. (*He closes his eyes*)

(ANNE *puts out her hand, wanting to shake hands*)

ANNE. Thank you. Thank you, Mr Dussel (*She taps him on the shoulder*)

(DUSSEL *jumps, terrified, then takes Anne's hand.*

Lighting Cue 17

As ANNE *vigorously shakes Dussel's hand, the lights dim quickly, except for a spot on Anne and Dussel.*

Lighting Cue 18

ANNE'S VOICE *comes to us dimly at first and then with increasing power. As she speaks, the spot quickly fades*)

ANNE'S VOICE. . . . and yesterday I finished Cissy Van Marxvelt's latest book. I think she is a first-class writer. I shall definitely let my children read her. Monday the twenty-first of September, nineteen forty-two. Mr Dussel and I had another battle yesterday. Yes, Mr Dussel. According to him, nothing—I repeat nothing—is right about me, my appearance, my character, my manners. While he was going on at me I thought— sometime I'll give you such a smack that you'll fly right up to the ceiling. Why is it that every grown-up thinks he knows the way to bring up children? Particularly the grown-ups that never

had any. I keep wishing Peter was a girl instead of a boy. Then
I would have someone to talk to. Margot's a darling, but she
takes everything too seriously. To pause for a moment on the
subject of Mrs Van Daan.

(*The voice begins to fade and the lights come slowly up*)

Lighting Cue 19

I must tell you that her attempts to flirt with father are getting
her nowhere. Pim, thank goodness, won't play.

SCENE 4

SCENE—*The same. September 1942. Midnight.*

When the LIGHTS *come up there is darkness except for a little light
coming through the skylight of the room* L, *and the faintest trace of a
cool glow, making it possible to distinguish the forms of* ANNE *in the
downstage bed of the room* R, DUSSEL *in the cot in the room* R, *and*
MR *and* MRS FRANK *asleep on the couch.* MRS FRANK *lies on the
seat section,* MR FRANK *on the shelf pulled out from the base. His
overcoat is thrown over him. Their heads are downstage.* MARGOT *is
asleep up* L *by the shelves with the curtain pulled across the foot of her
pallet.* PETER *is asleep on the bed in the room* L. *In the attic* MRS VAN
DAAN *is asleep in bed.* MR VAN DAAN, *in trousers and undershirt,
is moving quietly towards the head of the attic stairs. He strikes a
match to light his way but extinguishes it at once as he starts down.*

Effects Cue 17

*From outside we hear two drunken German soldiers singing "Lili
Marlene". A girl's high giggle is heard as the trio clumps unsteadily
away. As these voices fade away,* MR VAN DAAN *strikes another
match at the foot of the attic stairs, blows it out, and we hear him
open and close the food cupboard under the sink.*

Effects Cue 18

*Outside, we hear running footsteps approach on the cobblestones and
pass into the distance. We see* MR VAN DAAN'S *dim figure sneaking
back up the attic stairs.*

Effects Cue 19

*After a pause we hear the sound of heavy boots again as they run
by and fade away down the street.* MR VAN DAAN *is upstairs again
and all is quiet. Suddenly out of the silence and darkness, we hear*
ANNE *scream*)

ANNE (*screaming*) No! No! Don't—don't take me. (*She moans,
tossing and crying in her sleep*)

(*The others wake, terrified.* DUSSEL *sits up in bed, furious*)

DUSSEL. Shush! Anne! Anne, for God's sake, shush!

ANNE (*still in her nightmare*) Save me! Save me! (*She screams
and screams*)

(Dussel *gets out of bed, goes to* Anne *and tries to wake her*)

Dussel. For God's sake! Quiet! Quiet! You want someone to hear?

(Mrs Frank *gets out of bed, snatches up her shawl, rushes in to Anne, sits on her bed and takes her in her arms.* Mr Frank *hurriedly gets up and puts on his overcoat.* Margot, *terrified, sits up, then rushes over to get the footstool. She drags it up* c *so that she can reach the hanging lamp.* Peter *gets up and puts up his blackout curtain.*

Effects Cue 20

The sound of planes high overhead and ack-ack fire is heard)

Mrs Frank. Hush, darling, hush. It's all right.

(Dussel *blows his nose*)

There, there—my poor baby—my child. (*To Dussel*) Will you be kind enough to turn on the light, Mr Dussel?

Lighting Cue 20

(Dussel *switches on the pendant* r)

It's nothing, my darling. It was just a dream.

Lighting Cue 21

(Margot *turns on the pendant* c. Anne *gradually comes out of her nightmare, still trembling with horror.* Mr Frank *goes into the room* r *and peers out past the blackout curtain over the window. He must be sure that no-one in the street heard the screams.*

Lighting Cue 22

Peter *turns on the lamp in the room* l, *slips into his bath-robe and comes into the centre room on his way to the door* r)

Dussel (*to Mrs Frank*) Something must be done about that child, Mrs Frank. Yelling like that. Who knows but there's somebody on the street. She's endangering all our lives.

Lighting Cue 23

(Mr Van Daan *turns on the attic light and comes down the stairs.*

Lighting Cue 24

Margot *pulls on her bath-robe, crosses to the table* r *and switches on the lamp*)

Mrs Frank. Anne, darling. Little Anne.
Dussel. Every night she twists and turns. I don't sleep. I spend half my night shushing her. And now it's nightmares.

(Margot *and* Peter *move to the door* r. Mrs Van Daan *sits up in bed and waits fearfully.* Mr Frank *moves to Margot and Peter and indicates that everything is all right.* Peter *takes* Margot *back to her pallet*)

Mrs Frank (*to Anne*) You're here, safe, you see? Nothing has happened. Please, Mr Dussel, go back to bed. She'll be herself in a minute or two. Won't you, Anne?

(DUSSEL *collects his glasses, pillow and a book from the chest*)

DUSSEL. Thank you, but I'm going to the W.C. The one place where there's peace. (*He stalks into the centre room*)
MR VAN DAAN. What is it? What happened?
DUSSEL. A nightmare. She was having a nightmare.
MR VAN DAAN. I thought someone was murdering her.
DUSSEL. Unfortunately, no. (*He goes into the W.C.*)

(MR VAN DAAN *goes up the attic stairs and explains all to his wife.* MR FRANK *comes into the centre room*)

MR FRANK. Thank you, Peter. Go back to bed.

(PETER *goes into the room* L.

Lighting Cue 25

MR FRANK *follows him, turns out the lamp and looks out of the window.*

Lighting Cue 26

Then he goes back to the centre room, gets up on the stool and turns off the pendant C. PETER *takes down his blackout curtain, looks for planes for a while, then lies down on his bed in his bath-robe.* MARGOT *sits on her bed*)

MRS FRANK. Would you like some water?

(ANNE *shakes her head*)

Was it a very bad dream? Perhaps if you told me . . .?
ANNE. I'd rather not talk about it.
MRS FRANK. Poor darling. Try to sleep, then. I'll sit right here beside you until you fall asleep. (*She brings the stool from the dressing-table to Anne's bed*)
ANNE. You don't have to.
MRS FRANK. But I'd like to stay with you—very much. Really.
ANNE. I'd rather you didn't.

(MR FRANK *moves to the bed, stands listening to the planes for a moment, then sits on the upstage end of the bed*)

MRS FRANK. Good night, then. (*She leans down to kiss Anne*)

(ANNE *puts her arm across her face and turns away*)

(*She tries not to show her hurt and kisses Anne's arm instead*) You'll be all right? There's nothing that you want?
ANNE. Will you please ask father to come.
MRS FRANK (*after a second*) Of course, Anne, dear. (*She hurries into the centre room, fighting back her tears. She passes Mr Frank and stands below the table*)

Lighting Cue 27

(Mr Van Daan *turns off the attic light and he and* Mrs Van
Daan *settle down.*

Effects Cue 20a

The sound of the planes and ack-ack fire fades)

(*To Mr Frank*) She wants you.

Mr Frank (*crossing to his wife; sensing her hurt*)   Edith, dear.

Mrs Frank. It's all right. I thank God that at least she will
turn to you when she needs comfort. Go to her, Otto. She is still
shaking with fear.

(Mr Frank *hesitates*)

Go to her. (*She crosses to the bed*)

(Mr Frank *looks at his wife for a moment, then goes to the
shelves up* L, *gets a pill from a bottle, collects a cup and goes to the
sink for water.* Mrs Frank *sits on the foot of her bed, trying to keep
from sobbing aloud.* Margot *rises, moves to Mrs Frank, sits by her
and puts her arms around her*)

She wants nothing of me. She pulled away when I leaned down
to kiss her.

Margot. It's a phase—you heard father—most girls go
through it—they turn to their fathers at this age—they give all
their love to their fathers.

Mrs Frank. You weren't like this. You didn't shut me out.

Margot. She'll get over it.

(Mr Frank *goes into the room* R, *pulls the stool aside and places
the cup on it.* Anne *flings her arms around him, clinging to him.*
Margot *takes the shawl from Mrs Frank and smooths the bed.* Mrs
Frank *lies down.* Margot *sits beside her a moment, comforting her*)

Anne. Oh, Pim. I dreamed that they came to get us. The
Green Police. They broke down the door and grabbed me and
started to drag me out the way they did Jopie.

Mr Frank. I want you to take this pill.

Anne. What is it?

Mr Frank. Something to quiet you.

(Anne *takes the pill and drinks some water*)

Do you want me to read to you for a while?

Anne. No. Just sit with me for a minute.

(Mr Frank *sits on the edge of the bed beside Anne, and puts the
cup on the stool*)

Was I awful? Did I yell terribly loud? Do you think anyone
outside could have heard?

Lighting Cue 28

(Margot *rises and turns out the lamp* R, *then goes back to her bed*)

MR FRANK. No. No. Lie quietly now, Try to sleep.

(ANNE, *still overwrought, lies back*)

ANNE. I'm a terrible coward. I'm so disappointed in myself. I think I've conquered my fear—I think I'm really grown-up— and then something happens—and I run to you like a baby. I love you, Father. I don't love anyone but you.

MR FRANK (*reproachfully*) Anneline!

ANNE (*pushing herself up on her elbows*) It's true. I've been thinking about it for a long time. You're the only one I love.

MR FRANK. It's fine to hear you tell me that you love me. But I'd be much happier if you said you loved your mother as well— she needs your help so much—your love.

ANNE. We have nothing in common. She doesn't understand me. Whenever I try to explain my views on life to her she asks me if I'm constipated. (*She falls back*)

MR FRANK. You hurt her very much just now. She's crying. She's in there, crying.

ANNE. I can't help it. I only told the truth. I didn't want her here. (*With sudden remorse she sits up and clings to Mr Frank*) Oh, Pim, I was horrible, wasn't I? And the worst of it is, I can stand off and look at myself doing it and know it's cruel and yet I can't stop doing it. What's the matter with me? Tell me. Don't say it's just a phase. Help me.

MR FRANK. There is so little that we parents can do to help our children. We can only try to set a good example—point the way. The rest you must do yourself. You must build your own character.

ANNE. I'm trying. Really I am. (*She lies back, more relaxed*) Every night before I go to sleep I think back over all of the things I did that day that were wrong—like putting the wet mop in Mr Dussel's bed—and this thing now with mother. I say to myself, that was wrong. I make up my mind I'm never going to do that again. Never! Of course I may do something worse—but at least I'll never do *that* again. (*The medicine begins its work. She becomes relaxed and drowsy*) I have a nicer side, Father—a sweeter, nicer side. But I'm scared to show it. I'm afraid that people are going to laugh at me if I'm serious. So the mean Anne comes to the outside, and the good Anne stays on the inside and I keep on trying to switch them around and have the good Anne outside and the bad Anne inside and be what I'd like to be—and might be—if only—only . . . (*She falls asleep*)

(MR FRANK *rises quietly, places the cup on the dressing-table, goes to the door and turns to look at Anne once more.*

Lighting Cue 29

He turns out the pendant R *and comes into the centre room.* MRS FRANK *sits up in bed.*

Lighting Cue 30

ANNE'S VOICE *comes to us dimly at first, and then with increasing power. As she speaks, the* LIGHTS *dim quickly*)

ANNE'S VOICE. . . . the air raids are getting worse. They come over day and night. The noise is terrifying. Pim says it should be music to our ears. The more planes, the sooner will come the end of the war. Mrs Van Daan pretends to be a fatalist. What will be, will be. But when the planes come over, who is the most frightened? No-one else but Petronella. Monday, the ninth of November, nineteen forty-two. Wonderful news. The Allies have landed in Africa. Pim says that we can look for an early finish to the war. Just for fun he asked each of us what was the first thing we wanted to do when we got out of here. Mrs Van Daan longs to be home with her own things, her needlepoint chairs, the Bechstein piano her father gave her—the best that money could buy. Peter would like to go to a movie. Mr Dussel wants to get back to his dentist's drill. He's afraid he is losing his touch. For myself, there are so many things—to ride a bike again—to laugh till my belly aches—to have new clothes from the skin out——

(*The voice begins to fade and the* LIGHTS *come slowly up*)

Lighting Cue 31

—to have a hot tub filled to overflowing and wallow in it for hours—to be back in school with my friends . . .

SCENE 5

SCENE—*The same. December 1942. Night.*
    It is the first night of the Hanukkah celebration in December of that year, 1942. The table C, *with the table* R *to extend its length, has been placed in front of the couch. A tablecloth covers this and is set with a small bowl of sliced apples and walnuts, a small decanter of wine and a pitcher of water. At the upstage end there is a Menorah, improvised by Anne, and provided with the Shamos candle and one other candle. The pendant* C *and the table-lamp* C *are on, but the lighting is concentrated on the table area, suggesting a warm candlelight.*

When the LIGHTS *come up,* PETER *is sitting on the stool from the room* R, *at the downstage end of the couch.* MRS VAN DAAN *is seated on the downstage end of the couch.* MR VAN DAAN *is seated* C *of the couch with* MRS FRANK *on the upstage end.* MARGOT *sits in an upright chair opposite her mother.* DUSSEL *sits in an armchair below Margot and* ANNE *is on the footstool below Dussel.* MR FRANK *stands at the upstage end of the table. An armchair is at his place. The "family" are dressed in their best. The men wear hats.* PETER *wears his cap.* MR FRANK *lights the Shamos, or "servant candle" on the Menorah before him. He takes it and holds it up as he reads the blessing from a prayer-book.*

MR FRANK (*reading*) "Praised be Thou, Oh Lord our God,

Ruler of the universe, who has sanctified us with Thy command-
ments and bidden us kindle the Hanukkah lights. Praised be
Thou, Oh Lord our God, Ruler of the universe, who has wrought
wondrous deliverances for our fathers in days of old. Praised be
Thou, Oh Lord our God, Ruler of the universe, that Thou has
given us life and sustenance and brought us to this happy season."
Amen. (*He lights the one candle of the Menorah with the "servant
candle" as he continues*) "We kindle this Hanukkah light to celebrate
the great and wonderful deeds wrought through the zeal with
which God filled the hearts of the heroic Maccabees, two
thousand years ago. They fought against indifference, against
tyranny and oppression, and they restored our Temple to us.
May these lights remind us that we should ever look to God,
whence cometh our help." Amen.

ALL. Amen.

(MR FRANK *hands the prayer-book to* MRS FRANK *and sits as she
rises*)

MRS FRANK (*reading Psalm one hundred and twenty-one*)   "I lift up
mine eyes unto the mountains, from whence cometh my help.
My help cometh from the Lord who made heaven and earth. He
will not suffer thy foot to be moved. He that keepeth thee will not
slumber. He that keepeth Israel doth neither slumber nor sleep.
The Lord is thy keeper. The Lord is thy shade upon thy right
hand. The sun shall not smite thee by day, nor the moon by
night. The Lord shall keep thee from all evil. He shall keep thy
soul. The Lord shall guard thy going out and thy coming in,
from this time forth and for evermore." Amen.

ALL. Amen.

(MRS FRANK *returns the prayer-book to Mr Frank, then crosses to
the shelves up* L *and collects eight plates.* MARGOT *rises, crosses to the
shelves up* L *and collects eight glasses*)

DUSSEL (*rising and handing his hat to Mr Frank*)   That was very
moving.

ANNE (*pulling him back*)   It isn't over yet.

MRS VAN DAAN. Sit down! Sit down!

(MR FRANK *collects Mr Van Daan's hat and takes it with his own
and Dussel's and puts them on the mantelpiece, with the prayer-book.
He then sits at the head of the table.* PETER *puts his cap in his pocket.*
MR VAN DAAN *starts to eat*)

ANNE (*to Dussel*)   There's lots more, songs and presents.

DUSSEL. Presents?

MRS FRANK (*crossing to the table and sitting in her place*)   Not this
year, unfortunately. (*She distributes the plates around the table*)

MRS VAN DAAN. But always on Hanukkah everyone gives
presents—everyone.

Dussel. Like our St Nicholas' Day.

(*There is a chorus of "no's" from the others*)

Mrs Van Daan. No! Not like St Nicholas. What kind of a Jew are you that you don't know Hanukkah?

Mrs Frank (*to Dussel*) I remember particularly the candles. First one, as we have tonight. Then the second night you light two candles, then the next night, three—and so on until you have eight candles burning. When there are eight candles it is truly beautiful. (*She rises, crosses to the shelves up* L, *collects two cups, then returns to her seat*)

(Margot *places the glasses on the table, then resumes her seat.* Dussel *pours the wine.* Mrs Van Daan *waters hers and Peter's wine*)

Mrs Van Daan (*handing a glass to Peter*) And the potato pancakes.

(Mrs Frank *waters the rest of the glasses of wine*)

Mr Van Daan. Don't talk about them.

Mrs Van Daan. I make the best latkas you ever tasted.

Mrs Frank. Invite us all next year—in your own home.

Mr Frank. Please willing.

Mrs Van Daan. Please willing.

Margot (*rising*) What I remember best is the presents we used to get when we were little—eight days of presents—and each day they got better and better.

Mrs Frank. We are all here, alive. That is present enough.

Anne (*excitedly*) No, it isn't. I've got something . . . (*She jumps up and rushes towards the room* R)

Mrs Frank. What is it?

Anne. Presents. (*She darts into the room* R, *and hurriedly puts on a little party hat she has improvised from her lampshade; a paper flower and bits of ribbon cover it. An elastic goes under her chin. She snatches up her school satchel bulging with parcels and comes running back to* LC *where she puts the bag on the floor*)

Mrs Van Daan (*during this*) Presents!

(*A toast is led by* Mr Van Daan)

All. L'chaim, l'chaim!

Dussel (*pointing at Anne*) Look!

Mr Van Daan. What's she got on her head?

Peter. A lampshade.

Anne (*fumbling in the satchel*) Oh, dear. They're every which way. (*She pulls out a parcel at random. It is a thin book in a manila envelope, with a poem written on the outside. She is breathless with excitement*) This is for Margot. (*She moves between Margot and Mr Frank and hands the packet to Margot*) Read it out loud.

MARGOT (*reading*)

> "You have never lost your temper
> You never will, I fear,
> You are so good,
> But if you should,
> Put all your cross words here."

(*She slips the book out of the envelope*)

MRS FRANK (*half rising*) What is it?

MARGOT. A new crossword puzzle book. (*To Anne*) Where did you ever get it?

ANNE. It isn't new. It's one that you've done. But I rubbed it all out, and if you wait a little and forget you can do it all over again. (*She returns to her satchel*)

MARGOT (*resuming her seat*) It's wonderful, Anne. Thank you. You'd never know it wasn't new.

Effects Cue 21

(*From outside we hear the sound of a streetcar passing.* ANNE *takes a small wrapped bottle half filled with liquid from her satchel, crosses and stands between her mother and father*)

ANNE (*holding out the bottle*) Mrs Van Daan.

MRS VAN DAAN (*taking the bottle and unwrapping it*) This is awful—I haven't anything for anyone—I never thought . . .

MR FRANK. This is all Anne's idea.

MRS VAN DAAN (*holding up the bottle*) What is it?

ANNE. It's hair shampoo. I took all the odds and ends of soap and mixed them with the last of my toilet water.

MRS VAN DAAN. Oh, Anneke! (*She takes off the top, sniffs, then lets the others smell*)

ANNE (*returning to her satchel*) I wanted to write a poem for all of them, but I didn't have time. (*She takes out a shoebox, hides it behind her, and imitates Mr Van Daan's walk and voice as she returns to* R *of Mr Frank*) Yours, Mr Van Daan, is *really* something—something you want more than anything. (*She hands the box to Mr Van Daan and waits for him to open it*) Look! Cigarettes!

MR VAN DAAN (*taking out two dark brown cigarettes; delighted*) Cigarettes!

ANNE. Two of them. Pim found some old pipe tobacco in the pocket lining of his coat—and we made them—or rather, Pim did.

MRS VAN DAAN. Let me see. Well, look at that. Light it, Putti. Light it.

(MR VAN DAAN *hesitates, cigarette in hand, and looks suspiciously at Anne*)

ANNE (*reassuring him*) It's tobacco, really it is. There's a little fluff in it, but not much.

(*Everyone watches intently as* MR VAN DAAN *cautiously lights a cigarette*)

PETER. It works!

MRS VAN DAAN. Look at him!

(*The cigarette flares up. Everyone laughs as* MR VAN DAAN *coughs and chokes*)

MR VAN DAAN (*spluttering*) Thank you, Anne. Thank you.

(ANNE *rushes back to her satchel and takes a small piece of writing paper from it*)

ANNE (*crossing to Mrs Frank and handing her the paper*) For Mother, Hanukkah greeting. (*She pulls Mrs Frank to her feet*)

MRS FRANK (*reading*)
> "Here's an I.O.U. that I promise to pay.
> Ten hours of doing whatever you say.
> Signed, Anne Frank."

(*Touched, she takes Anne in her arms and holds her close*)

DUSSEL (*to Anne*) Ten hours of doing what you're told? *Anything* you're told?

ANNE. That's right. (*She returns to her satchel*)

DUSSEL (*after thinking it over for a second*) You wouldn't want to sell that, Mrs Frank?

MRS FRANK. Never! This is the most precious gift I've ever had. (*She sits and shows the piece of paper to the others*)

(ANNE *pulls out a scarf, the same scarf we saw in the first scene and crosses to* L *of Mr Frank*)

ANNE. For Pim.

MR FRANK. Anneke—I wasn't supposed to have a present. (*He takes the scarf, unfolds it, shows it to the others, then puts it on and tucks it inside his jacket*)

ANNE. It's a muffler—to put around your neck. I made it myself out of odds and ends—I knitted it in the dark each night, after I'd gone to bed. (*Ruefully*) I'm afraid it looks better in the dark. (*She gets Peter's and Mouschi's presents from her satchel, then returns to* L *of Mr Frank*)

MR FRANK. It's fine. It fits me perfectly. Thank you, Anneke.

ANNE (*going to Peter and handing him a ball of paper with a ribbon and little bells attached to it*) That's for Mouschi.

PETER (*rising and bowing*) On behalf of Mouschi, I thank you. (*He resumes his seat*)

ANNE (*handing Peter a small package; hesitantly*) And—this is yours—from Mrs Quack Quack.

(PETER *holds the little case gingerly in his hands*)

Well—open it. Aren't you going to open it? (*Impatient and excited, she moves* C *behind Dussel*)

PETER. I'm scared to. I know something's going to jump out and hit me.

ANNE. No. It's nothing like that, really.

(PETER *opens the case*)

MRS VAN DAAN. What is it, Peter? Go on, Show it.

ANNE (*excitedly*) It's a safety razor.

DUSSEL. A what?

ANNE. A razor.

MRS VAN DAAN. You didn't make that out of odds and ends.

ANNE (*to Peter*) Miep got it for me. It's not new. It's second-hand. But you really do need a razor, now.

DUSSEL (*peering at Peter*) For what?

ANNE (*pointing to Peter*) Look on his upper lip—you can see the beginning of a moustache.

DUSSEL. He wants to get rid of that? Put a little milk on it and let the cat lick it off.

PETER (*rising and crossing to the room* L) Think you're funny, don't you?

DUSSEL. Look! He can't wait. He's going in to try it.

PETER. I'm going in to give Mouschi his present. (*He goes into the room* L, *slams the door behind him, sits on the window-seat with his back to the audience, rolls up a towel and tucks it into his jacket*)

MR VAN DAAN (*disgustedly*) Mouschi, Mouschi, Mouschi.

Effects Cue 22

(*In the distance we hear a dog persistently barking.* ANNE *brings a gift to Dussel*)

ANNE. And last but never least, my room-mate, Mr Dussel.

(DUSSEL, *surprised, swings his chair so that he is nearly facing front*)

DUSSEL. For me? You have something for me?

(ANNE *hands a tiny box to* DUSSEL, *who beams and opens it*)

ANNE. I made them myself.

DUSSEL (*puzzled*) Capsules! Two capsules.

ANNE (*excitedly*) They're ear-plugs.

DUSSEL. Ear-plugs?

ANNE. To put in your ears so you won't hear me when I thrash around at night. I saw them advertised in a magazine. They're not real ones—I made them out of cotton and candle wax. Try them—see if they don't work—see if you can hear me talk.

DUSSEL (*putting a capsule in his right ear*) Wait now until I get them in—(*he puts a capsule in his left ear*) so.

ANNE. Are you ready?

DUSSEL. Huh?

ANNE (*louder*) Are you ready?

Dussel (*rising with an agonized look on his face*) Good God! They've gone inside. (*He crosses to* LC, *thumping his head and trying frantically to get out the ear plugs*)

(*Everyone laughs except* ANNE, *who is chagrined at the turn of events*)

I can't get them out. (*Finally he gets them out and stands up* R *of Mr Frank*) Thank you, Anne. Thank you. (*He pockets the plugs*)

Mr Van Daan ⎫   ⎧ A real Hanukkah!
Mrs Van Daan ⎬ (*together*) ⎨ Wasn't it cute of her?
Mrs Frank   ⎪   ⎪ I don't know when she did it.
Margot   ⎭   ⎩ I love my present.

Anne (*sitting in her place*) And now let's have the song, Father —please. (*To Dussel*) Have you heard the Hanukkah song, Mr Dussel? The song is the whole thing. (*She sings enthusiastically*)

"Oh, Hanukkah, Oh, Hanukkah.
A sweet celebration . . ."

Mr Frank (*quietening Anne*) I'm afraid, Anne, we shouldn't sing that song tonight. (*To Dussel*) It's a song of jubilation, of rejoicing. One is apt to become too enthusiastic.

Anne. Oh, please, please. Let's sing the song. I promise not to shout.

(Peter *rises and comes into the centre room, ostentatiously holding a bulge in his coat as if he were holding his cat, and dangling Mouschi's present before it*)

Mr Frank. Very well. But quietly now—I'll keep an eye on you, and when . . .

(Dussel *points at Peter and begins to wheeze and cough*)

Dussel. You—you. How many times . . . I told you . . . Out! Out!

(Mr Van Daan *rises, brushes past his wife and strides to Peter*)

Mr Van Daan. What's the matter with you? Haven't you any sense? Get that cat out of here.

Peter (*innocently*) Cat?

Mr Van Daan. You heard me. Get it out of here.

Peter. I have no cat. (*Delighted with his joke, he pulls the towel from his coat and holds it high for all to see*)

(*The group at the table laugh, enjoying the joke.* Peter *puts the ball and towel on the shelves up* L)

Dussel (*still wheezing*) It doesn't need to be the cat—his clothes are enough—(*he coughs unconvincingly to prove his point*) when he comes out of that room . . .

Mr Van Daan (*crossing to Dussel*) Don't worry. You won't be bothered any more. We're getting rid of it.

Dussel. At last you listen to me. (*He goes into the room* R)

Mr Van Daan (*calling after him*) I'm not doing it for you. That's all in your mind—all of it.

(Dussel *takes a swallow of his medicine then sits on his bed to recover*)

(*He circles below the table to his place*) I'm doing it because I'm sick of seeing that cat eat all our food.

Peter (*crossing to* L *of the table*) That's not true. I only give him bones—scraps . . .

Mr Van Daan (*standing at his place*) Don't tell me! He gets fatter every day. Damn cat looks better than any of us. Out he goes tonight. (*He sits*)

Peter. No! No!

Anne (*rising from her stool and sitting in Dussel's chair; defending Peter*) Mr Van Daan, you can't do that. That's Peter's cat. Peter loves that cat.

Mrs Frank (*quietly*) Anne.

Peter (*an ultimatum*) If he goes, I go.

Mr Van Daan (*unworried*) Go! Go!

Mrs Van Daan (*putting a finish to the argument*) You're not going and the cat's not going.

(Peter *moves up* L)

Now, please—this is Hanukkah—Hanukkah—this is the time to celebrate—what's the matter with all of you? Come on, Anne. Let's have the song.

Anne (*singing spiritedly*)
        "Oh, Hanukkah. Oh, Hanukkah.
        The sweet celebration . . ."

Mr Frank (*rising and interrupting*) I think we should first blow out the candle——

(Margot *makes a little sound of protest*)

(*He explains further*)—then we'll have something for tomorrow night.

Margot. But, Father, you're supposed to let them burn themselves out.

Mr Frank. I'm sure that God understands shortages.

(Peter *moves and stands behind Margot's chair*)

(*He prays*) "Praised be Thou, Oh Lord our God, who hast sustained us and permitted us to celebrate this joyous festival." Amen. (*He leans forward to blow out the candles*)

Effects Cue 23

(*There is a sudden crash of something falling below.*

Effects Cue 24

The dog starts to bark again. They all freeze in horror, motionless, straining to hear. For a few seconds there is complete silence, then Mrs Frank *snatches off her shoes, rises and moves swiftly to the table-lamp* c.

Lighting Cue 32

Mrs Frank *switches off the lamp.* Mr Frank *hurries to the head of the stair-well.* Mr Van Daan *rises and follows him. All take off their shoes.* Mr Frank *signals to Peter to turn off the pendant* c. Mrs Frank *moves up* lc. Peter *cannot reach the chain so he pulls the chair from up* r *to a position under the lamp, and stands on it. Just as he is touching the lamp he loses his balance. The chair goes out from under him. He falls. The iron shade crashes to the floor.*

Lighting Cue 33

The light of the pendant c *goes out.*

Effects Cue 25

There is the sound of feet below, running down the stairs. Peter *picks himself up immediately*)

Mr Van Daan (*moving to Peter; under his breath*)   God Almighty!

(Dussel *rises, comes to the door of the room* r, *and moves towards Peter, gesturing for silence.* Margot *rises.* Anne *rises and moves* lc. Mr Van Daan *listens intently. The footsteps die away. The following lines are whispered*)

Do you hear anything?

(Mr Frank *listens carefully for another moment*)

Mr Frank. No. I think they've gone.

(Mrs Van Daan *rises and stands down* r *of the table*)

Mrs Van Daan (*with a trace of hysteria in her voice*) It's the Green Police. They've found us.

Mr Frank. If they had, they wouldn't have left. They'd be up here by now.

Mrs Van Daan. I know it's the Green Police. They've gone to get help. That's all. They'll be back.

Mr Van Daan. Or it may have been the Gestapo, looking for papers.

Mr Frank. Or a thief, looking for money.

Mrs Van Daan. We've got to do something. Quick! Quick! Before they come back.

Mr Van Daan. There isn't anything to do. Just wait.

(Mr Frank *holds up his hand for them to be quiet, and listens intently. There is complete silence as they all strain to hear any sound from below. Suddenly* Anne *begins to sway. With a low cry she falls to the floor in a faint.* Mrs Frank *goes quickly to Anne and sits on the floor, lifting Anne's head on to her lap*)

Mrs Frank. Get some water, please. Get some water.

(Margot *moves towards the sink*)

Mr Van Daan (*grabbing Margot*) No. No. No-one's going to run water.

Mr Frank. If they've found us, they've found us. Get the water.

(Margot *continues to the sink*)

(*He moves to the shelves up* L *and picks up a torch*) I'm going down.

(Margot *rushes to* Mr Frank *and clings to him as he moves to the stair-well.* Anne *struggles back to consciousness*)

Margot. No, Father, no. There may be someone there, waiting—it may be a trap.

Mr Frank. This is Saturday. There is no way for us to know what has happened until Miep or Mr Kraler come on Monday morning. We cannot live with this uncertainty.

Margot. Don't go, Father.

Mrs Frank. Hush, darling, hush.

(Mr Frank *shakes Margot off and exits quietly down the stair-well*)

Margot. Stay close to me.

(Margot *goes to Mrs Frank*)

Mr Van Daan. Shush! Shush! (*He crosses and stands down* R)

(Margot *remembers the water, gets some from the sink, then kneels* L *of Mrs Frank and gives Anne a sip*)

Mrs Van Daan (*becoming hysterical*) Putti, where's our money? Get our money. I hear you can buy the Green Police off, so much a head. Go upstairs, quick. Get the money.

Mr Van Daan. Keep still.

Mrs Van Daan (*pleading*) Do you want to be dragged off to a concentration camp? Are you going to stand there and wait for them to come up and get you? (*She sinks to her knees in front of her husband as her hysteria mounts*) Do something, I tell you.

Mr Van Daan. Will you keep still! (*He shoves her aside and crosses quietly and quickly to the stair-well and listens*)

(Mrs Van Daan *falls sobbing against the couch.* Peter *hurries to her and helps her to sit on the couch. There is a second of silence, then* Anne *can stand it no longer*)

Anne. Someone go after father. Make father come back.

(Mrs Frank *covers Anne's mouth to muffle her voice*)

PETER (*hurrying to the stair-well*) I'll go.

MR VAN DAAN (*pushing Peter roughly up* L) Haven't you done enough?

(PETER *grabs a chair as if to hit Mr Van Daan with it, then puts it down and buries his face in his hands*)

ANNE. Please, please, Mr Van Daan. Get father.

MR VAN DAAN. Quiet! Quiet!

(ANNE *is shocked into silence.* MRS FRANK *pulls Anne closer, holding her protectively in her arms*)

MRS FRANK (*praying softly*) "I lift up mine eyes unto the mountains, from whence cometh my help. My help cometh from the Lord who made heaven and earth. He will not suffer thy foot to be moved. He that keepeth thee will not slumber . . ." (*She breaks off as she hears someone coming*)

(*They all watch the stair-well tensely.*
MR FRANK *enters up the stair-well.* ANNE *rises, rushes to Mr Frank and holds him tightly.* MRS FRANK *and* MARGOT *rise*)

MR FRANK. It was a thief. That noise must have scared him away.

(MR VAN DAAN *crosses below Mrs Frank and Margot, then goes up* C *and begins pacing back and forth across the room*)

MRS VAN DAAN. Thank God!

MR FRANK. He took the cash box. And the radio. He ran away in such a hurry that he didn't stop to shut the street door. It was swinging wide open.

(*A breath of relief sweeps over the others*)

I think it'd be good to have some light.

MARGOT. Are you sure it's all right?

MR FRANK. The danger has passed.

Lighting Cue 34

(MARGOT *goes to the table-lamp* C *and switches it on*)

Don't be so terrified, Anne. We're safe.

DUSSEL (*crossing to Mr Frank; sharply and tensely*) Who says the danger has passed? Don't you realize we are in greater danger than ever?

MR FRANK. Mr Dussel, will you be still. (*He leads Anne to the table, sits her in Margot's chair, then sits in his own chair above the table and tries to calm her*)

DUSSEL (*pointing to Peter*) Thanks to this clumsy fool, there's someone now who knows we're up here. Someone now knows we're up here, hiding.

MRS VAN DAAN (*rising and crossing below the table to Dussel*) Someone knows we're here, yes. But who is the someone? A thief. A thief. You think a thief is going to go to the Green Police and say—I was robbing a place the other night and I heard a noise up over my head? You think a thief is going to do that?

DUSSEL. Yes. I think he will.

MRS VAN DAAN (*hysterically*) You're crazy. (*She stumbles back to her seat at the table*)

(PETER *follows protectively, pushes Dussel aside, then sits on his stool down* R *and comforts his mother*)

DUSSEL (*continuing to Mrs Van Daan*) I think some day he'll be caught and then he'll make a bargain with the Green Police— if they'll let him off, he'll tell them where some Jews are hiding. (*He goes into the room* R *and sinks down on to his bed*)

MR VAN DAAN. He's right.

(MRS FRANK *crosses to her place at the table*)

ANNE (*terrified*) Father, let's get out of here. We can't stay here now. Let's go.

MR VAN DAAN. Go! Where?

MRS FRANK (*sinking into her place at the table; in despair*) Yes. Where?

(MR FRANK *rises quickly and surveys the "family" as they slump in their places. He knows he must restore their courage.* MR VAN DAAN *crosses to Anne's stool, where he sits facing* R)

MR FRANK. Have we lost all faith? All courage? A moment ago we thought that they'd come for us. We were sure it was the end. But it wasn't the end. We're alive, safe. (*He prays*) We thank Thee, Oh Lord our God, that in Thy infinite mercy Thou hast again seen fit to spare us.

Lighting Cue 35

(*He blows out the candles, then turns to Anne*) Come on, Anne. The song. The song.

(ANNE *starts falteringly to sing. Her voice is hardly audible at first*)

ANNE (*singing*)
              "Oh, Hanukkah. Oh, Hanukkah.
              The sweet celebration."

(*As she goes on singing, one by one the others join in. There is no unity, no rhythm at first.* MARGOT *moves slowly to* L *of Mr Frank.* MRS VAN DAAN *sobs as she sings.* DUSSEL *rises and comes out of the room* R. MARGOT *draws him into the group. As they sing, "Many are the reasons for good cheer", their courage and faith are beginning to return*)

ALL (*singing*)
> "Around the feast we gather
> In complete jubilation.
> Happiest of seasons
> Now is here.
> Many are the reasons for good cheer.
> Together
> We'll weather
> Whatever tomorrow may bring."

Lighting Cue 36

(*The* LIGHTS *commence to dim in rhythm to the phrase accents. They sing on with growing courage*)

> "So hear us rejoicing
> And merrily voicing
> The Hanukkah song that we sing.
> Hoy!"

(*The* LIGHTS BLACK-OUT *and the* CURTAIN *starts to slowly fall as they sing on*)

> "Hear us rejoicing
> And merrily voicing
> The Hanukkah song that we sing."

CURTAIN

ACT II

SCENE I

SCENE—*The same. January 1944. Late afternoon.*
Slight changes are evident in the rooms. A faded floral print covers the lower half of the W.C. window in the room R. *A stained antimacassar covers the back of the couch in the centre room. One armchair is down* L, *and a line of washing is stretched across the room.*

Before the CURTAIN *rises,* ANNE'S VOICE *is heard reading from the diary.*

ANNE'S VOICE. Saturday, the first of January, nineteen forty-four. Another new year has begun and we find ourselves still in our hiding place. We have been here now for one year, five months, and twenty-five days. It seems that our life is at a standstill.

When the CURTAIN *rises, the stage is in darkness.* ANNE'S VOICE *goes on without a break, and continues until the* LIGHTS *are full up.*

Lighting Cue 37

A spot comes up on ANNE *sitting* R *of the table* C, *writing in her diary.*

Lighting Cue 38

After a moment, the scene lights build around this area. It is late afternoon of a cold Winter day. In the centre room MRS FRANK, *in sweater, apron and fingerless gloves, takes down the laundry and exits with it above the kitchen area.* MR FRANK, *also in a sweater, sits reading in his armchair at the extreme down* L *corner of the room. His back is three-quarters to the audience.* MARGOT *lies on the couch with a blanket over her and the many-coloured knitted scarf around her throat.* PETER *sits under the skylight in the room* L, *reading. He is wearing his suit jacket with the collar turned up and a knitted cap. The* VAN DAANS *are in the attic room.* MRS VAN DAAN *is wearing Peter's raincoat.* MR VAN DAAN *is in sweater and gloves.* DUSSEL *lies asleep on his bed in the room* R.

We are all a little thinner. The Van Daans' "discussions" are as violent as ever. Mother still does not understand me. But then I don't understand her, either. There is one great change, however, A change in myself. I read somewhere that girls of my age don't feel quite certain of themselves. That they become quiet within and begin to think of the miracle that is taking place in their bodies. I think that what is happening to me is so wonderful—

not only what can be seen, but what is taking place inside. Each time it has happened I have a feeling that I have a——

(ANNE'S VOICE *hesitates a second.* ANNE *looks up, thinking of the proper phrase. She finds it and continues writing*)

—sweet secret.

Effects Cue 26

(*We hear the carillon chimes begin a hymn.* ANNE'S VOICE *fades slowly*)

And in spite of my pain, I long for the time when I shall feel that secret within me again.

(*There is a pause.*

Effects Cue 27

The pause is broken by Miep's signal on the door buzzer. Everyone is momentarily startled. MRS FRANK *hurries anxiously back into the centre room*)

MR FRANK (*rising; reassuringly for Mrs Frank's benefit*) It's Miep. (*He goes quickly down the stairs to unbolt the door*)

(MRS FRANK *calls upstairs to the Van Daans, then crosses and knocks on the door* L *on her way to the stair-well*)

MRS FRANK. Wake up, everyone. Miep is here.

Lighting Cue 39

(*The spot fades on* ANNE, *who quickly finishes writing, rises, puts her diary under her arm and stands below the table* C. MARGOT *sits up, pulling the blankets around her.* DUSSEL, *disgruntled, sits on the edge of his bed, listening.*

MIEP *enters up the stairs. She carries a small bunch of flowers and a bag of food.*

KRALER *follows Miep on. He carries a small package and a bunch of flowers. They are both bundled up against the cold*)

Miep—and Mr Kraler—what a delightful surprise.

(MIEP, *after giving a warm greeting and the bag of food to Mrs Frank, crosses below her to* ANNE *and they affectionately embrace.* PETER *rises and comes into the centre room*)

KRALER (*giving the package to Mrs Frank*) We came to bring you New Year's greetings.

MRS FRANK. You shouldn't—you should have at least one day to yourselves. (*She crosses above the table and places the package on the mantelpiece*)

(KRALER *moves up* L *and greets Peter*)

ANNE. Don't say that, it's so wonderful to see them. (*She sniffs at Miep's coat*) I can smell the wind and the cold on your clothes.

C

MIEP (*giving Anne the flowers*) There you are. (*She crosses to Margot and feels her forehead*) How are you, Margot? Feeling any better?

MARGOT. I'm all right.

ANNE. We filled her full of every kind of pill so she won't cough and make a noise. (*She runs into the room* R, *puts the diary into the window-seat, takes a glass of water from the chest of drawers, puts her flowers in it, then puts them on the dressing-table*)

Effects Cue 28

(*The carillon hymn finishes.* ANNE *comes into the centre room and sits* R *of the table. The* VAN DAANS *come down the attic stairs.*

Effects Cue 29

Outside there is the sound of a band playing)

MRS VAN DAAN. Well, hello, Miep. Mr Kraler.

KRALER (*moving to Mrs Van Daan and giving her the flowers*) With my hope for peace in the New Year.

(MIEP *acknowledges the* VAN DAANS' *greetings then moves below the table.* PETER *moves down* L *of the table and meets Miep* C)

PETER. Miep, have you seen Mouschi? Have you seen him anywhere around?

MIEP. I'm sorry, Peter. I asked everyone in the neighbourhood had they seen a grey cat. But they said "no".

(PETER *moves down* L. MRS VAN DAAN *places her flowers in the sink.*

MR FRANK *comes up the stairs. He carries two books and a small cake on a plate, inscribed "Peace in 1944")*

MR FRANK. Look what Miep's brought for us. (*He places the cake on the table*)

MRS FRANK (*moving above the table*) A cake!

MR VAN DAAN. A cake! (*He circles the table from* R *to Miep, gaily pinches her cheeks, and continues around the table to the shelves up* L) I'll get some plates.

(DUSSEL *hastily puts on a coat, rises and comes into the centre room.* MR FRANK *crosses above the table, puts the books on the mantelpiece, then crosses and talks to Kraler.* MIEP *crosses to the stair-well*)

MRS FRANK. Thank you, Miepia. You shouldn't have done it. You must have used all of your sugar ration for weeks.

(MRS VAN DAAN *moves to* R *of Mrs Frank*)

(*She picks up the cake and hands it to Mrs Van Daan*) It's beautiful, isn't it?

MRS VAN DAAN (*to Miep*) It's been ages since I even saw a cake. Not since you brought us one last year. (*She moves below the right end of the table*)

(MRS FRANK *gets the teapot from the draining-board, goes to the stove, pours hot water into the teapot, then brings it to the table*)

Remember? Don't you remember, you gave us one on New Year's Day? Just this time last year? I'll never forget it because you had "Peace in nineteen forty-three" on it. (*She looks at the cake and reads*) "Peace in nineteen forty-four."

MIEP. Well, it has to come sometime, you know. (*She looks across at Dussel*) Hello, Mr Dussel. (*She crosses quickly to Dussel, shakes hands with him, then goes down* L)

(MRS FRANK *brings four cups from the draining-board and puts them on the table.* DUSSEL *moves up* C)

KRALER (*to Dussel*)   How are you? (*He shakes hands with Dussel*)

(MR VAN DAAN *brings plates, forks and a knife from the shelves up* L *and puts them on the table*)

MR VAN DAAN (*to his wife*)   Here's the knife, liefje. Now, how many of us are there?

MIEP   ⎫(*together*)   ⎧None for me, thank you.
KRALER ⎭   ⎩No, thanks.

MR FRANK. Oh, please. You must.

MIEP. I couldn't.

MR VAN DAAN. Good!

(MRS FRANK *gets four more cups from the draining-board and puts them on the table.* MRS VAN DAAN *crosses to* L *of the table, places the cake on it and sits*)

That leaves one—two—three—seven of us.

DUSSEL (*moving down* R *of the table and pointing to himself*)   Eight! Eight! It's the same number as it always is.

MR VAN DAAN. I left Margot out. I take it for granted Margot won't eat any.

ANNE. Why wouldn't she?

MRS FRANK (*pouring tea*)   I think it won't harm her.

MR VAN DAAN. All right. All right. I just didn't want her to start coughing again, that's all.

DUSSEL. And please, Mrs Frank should cut the cake.

MR VAN DAAN   ⎫   ⎧What's the difference?
MRS VAN DAAN ⎬(*together*) ⎨It's not Mrs Frank's cake, is it,
                       ⎭   ⎩   Miep? It's for all of us.

DUSSEL. Mrs Frank divides things better.

(MRS VAN DAAN *rises and moves below the table*)

MRS VAN DAAN⎫(*together*)   ⎧What are you trying to say?
MR VAN DAAN ⎭   ⎩Oh, come on. Stop wasting time.

(MRS VAN DAAN *strides across to* DUSSEL, *who retreats two steps up* R. MRS FRANK *returns the teapot to the draining-board*)

MRS VAN DAAN (*confronting Dussel*) Don't I always give everybody exactly the same? Don't I?

MR VAN DAAN. Forget it, Kerli.

MRS VAN DAAN (*overlapping*) No. I want an answer. (*To Dussel*) Don't I?

DUSSEL. Yes. Yes. Everybody gets exactly the same——

(MRS VAN DAAN, *satisfied, turns away to the cake*)

—except Mr Van Daan always gets a little bit more.

(*The* VAN DAANS *whirl and come back at Dussel,* MR VAN DAAN *holding the knife.* DUSSEL *retreats before their onslaught to the W.C. steps.* MRS FRANK *returns to the table, picks up a cup of tea and hands it to Miep*)

MR VAN DAAN. That's a lie. She always cuts the same.

MR FRANK. Please, please. (*He moves to Miep. Apologetically*) You see what a little sugar cake does to us? It goes right to our heads.

MR VAN DAAN (*handing the knife to Mrs Frank*) Here you are, Mrs Frank.

(MR FRANK *crosses and stands below the table, to help Mrs Frank*)

MRS FRANK. Thank you. (*To Miep*) Are you sure you won't have some? (*She cuts the cake*)

MIEP. No, really, I have to go in a minute. (*She drinks her tea*)

PETER (*moving to Miep*) Maybe Mouschi went back to our house—they say that cats . . . Do you ever get over there? I mean —do you suppose you could . . .?

(*The* VAN DAANS *come to* L *of Mrs Frank and* MR VAN DAAN *snatches the first piece of cake.* MRS VAN DAAN *gets the second piece on a plate and takes it to the stove, where she stands and eats*)

MIEP. I'll try, Peter. The first minute I get I'll try. But I'm afraid, with him gone a week . . .

DUSSEL. Make up your mind, already someone has had a nice big dinner from that cat.

(PETER *is furious and inarticulate. He starts towards Dussel as if to hit him.* MR FRANK *restrains Peter.* MRS FRANK *speaks quickly to Miep to ease the situation*)

MRS FRANK. This is delicious, Miep. (*She hands cake to Dussel*)

MRS VAN DAAN. Delicious!

(MR VAN DAAN *sits in the chair above the stair-well and wolfs his cake.* PETER *moves up* L. MR FRANK *moves to* R *of* MRS FRANK, *who hands cake to him and Anne*)

MR VAN DAAN. Dirk's in luck to get a girl who can bake like this.

MIEP (*putting her empty cup on the table*)   I have to run. Dirk's taking me to a party tonight.

(MRS FRANK *takes cake to Margot, then puts the remaining pieces on plates*)

ANNE (*to Miep*)   How heavenly! Remember now what everyone is wearing, and what you have to eat and everything, so you can tell us tomorrow.

MIEP.   I'll give you a full report. Good-bye, everyone. (*She turns to the stair-well*)

MR VAN DAAN (*to Miep*)   Just a minute. (*He rises*) There's something I'd like you to do for me. (*He hurries up the stairs to the attic room*)

MRS VAN DAAN (*looking fearfully after her husband; sharply*)   Putti, where are you going? (*She starts after him, calling hysterically*) What do you want? Putti, what are you going to do? (*She rushes up the stairs after him*)

MIEP (*to Peter*)   What's wrong?

PETER (*his sympathy with his mother*)   Father says he's going to sell her fur coat. She's crazy about that old fur coat.

DUSSEL.   Is it possible? Is it possible that anyone is so silly as to worry about a fur coat in times like this?

(PETER *advances on Dussel but is restrained by* MR FRANK. MRS FRANK *sits above the table on the padded stool*)

PETER (*to Dussel*)   It's none of your darn business—and if you say one more thing—I'll—I'll take you and I'll . . . I mean it—I'll . . .

(*Suddenly there is a piercing scream from* MRS VAN DAAN *in the attic room. She grabs at the fur coat as* MR VAN DAAN *passes her to go downstairs with it*)

MRS VAN DAAN.   No! No! No! Don't you dare take that. You hear? It's mine.

(PETER, *embarrassed and miserable, goes to the stairs but can do nothing*)

My father gave me that. You didn't give it to me. You have no right. Let go of it—you hear?

(MR VAN DAAN *pulls the coat from her hands and hurries down the attic stairs. As he comes into the centre room the others look away, embarrassed for him.* MRS VAN DAAN, *sobbing, sinks on to the attic floor*)

MR VAN DAAN (*to Kraler*)   Just a little—discussion over the advisability of selling this coat. As I have often reminded Mrs Van Daan, it's very selfish of her to keep it when people outside are in such desperate need of clothing. (*He gives the coat to Miep*) So if you will please to sell it for us? It should fetch a good price.

 (MIEP *turns to go*)

(*With an afterthought*) And, by the way, will you get me cigarettes? I don't care what kind they are—get all you can.

 MIEP. It's terribly difficult to get them, Mr Van Daan. But I'll try. Good-bye.

 MRS FRANK. Good-bye.

 MR FRANK. Good-bye, Miep.

 (MIEP *exits down the stairs.* MR FRANK *follows her down the steps and bolts the door after her.* MRS FRANK *rises and gives Kraler a cup of tea*)

 MRS FRANK. Are you sure you won't have some cake, Mr Kraler?

 KRALER (*with a step towards Mrs Frank*) I'd better not.

 MR VAN DAAN (*moving to L of Kraler*) You're still feeling badly? What does the doctor say?

 KRALER. I haven't been to him.

 MRS FRANK. Now, Mr Kraler . . .

 KRALER (*sitting L of the table*) Oh, I tried. But you can't get near a doctor these days—they're so busy. After weeks I finally managed to get one on the telephone. I told him I'd like an appointment—I wasn't feeling very well. You know what he answers—over the telephone—"Stick out your tongue".

 (*They laugh.*
  MR FRANK *enters up the stairs and sits in the armchair down* L.
 MR VAN DAAN *takes a cup of tea and moves to the fireplace.* MRS FRANK *gives a cup of tea to Dussel and cake and tea to* PETER, *who sits on the W.C. steps to eat*)

(*He turns to Mr Frank*) I have some contracts here—I wonder if you'd look over them with me.

 MR FRANK (*holding out his hand*) Of course.

 KRALER (*rising*) If we could go downstairs . . .

 (MR FRANK *rises and goes down the stairs*)

(*He turns to the others*) Will you forgive us? I won't keep him a minute. (*He moves to the stairs*)

 MARGOT (*with sudden foreboding*) What's happened? Something's happened. Hasn't it, Mr Kraler?

 (KRALER *stops and turns, moves below the table and tries to reassure Margot with a pretence of casualness*)

 KRALER. No, really. I want your father's advice . . .

 MARGOT. Something's gone wrong. I know it.

Mr Frank (*coming back; to Kraler*) If it's something that concerns us here, it's better that we all hear it.

Kraler (*turning to Mr Frank; quietly*) But—the children . . .?

Mr Frank. What they'd imagine would be worse than any reality. (*He sits in the armchair down* l)

(Kraler *is reluctant, but begins his story. They all listen with intense apprehension and move slowly to sit.* Mrs Frank *sits above the table.* Mr Van Daan *sits on the upstage end of the couch.* Dussel *puts his cup and plate on the mantelpiece, then steps towards* c. Peter *rises and moves in*)

Kraler. It's a man in the storeroom. (*As he speaks to Mr Frank he circles* l *to above the chair* l *of the table*) I don't know whether or not you remember him—Carl, about fifty, heavy-set, near-sighted. He came with us just before you left.

Effects Cue 29a

(*The sound of the band fades*)

Mr Frank. He was from Utrecht?

Kraler. That's the man. A couple of weeks ago, when I was in the storeroom, he closed the door and asked me: "How's Mr Frank? What do you hear from Mr Frank?" I told him I only knew there was a rumour that you were in Switzerland. He said he'd heard that rumour, too, but he thought I might know something more. I didn't pay any attention to it—but then a thing happened yesterday. He'd brought some invoices to the office for me to sign. As I was going through them, I looked up. He was standing staring at the bookcase—(*he indicates the door at the foot of the stair-well*) the bookcase that hides your door. He said he thought he remembered a door there—wasn't there a door there that used to go up to the loft? Then he told me he wanted more money. Twenty guilders more a week. (*He sits* l *of the table*)

(Mrs Van Daan *rises, comes slowly down the attic steps and sits on the bottom step, listening*)

Mr Van Daan (*bursting out*) Blackmail!

Mr Frank (*calmly*) Twenty guilders? Very modest blackmail.

Mr Van Daan. That's just the beginning.

Dussel (*nervously rushing down* l *of the table; to Mr Frank*) You know what I think? He was the thief who was down there that night. That's how he knows we're here. (*He returns up* rc)

Mr Frank (*to Kraler*) How was it left? What did you tell him?

Kraler. I said I had to think about it. What shall I do? Pay him the money—take a chance on firing him—or what? I don't know.

Dussel (*crossing to* lc; *more agitated*) For God's sake don't fire him. Pay him what he asks—keep him here where you can have your eye on him.

Mr Frank (*to Mr Kraler*)   Is it so much that he's asking? What are they paying nowadays?

(Dussel *moves up* c)

Kraler. He could get it in a war plant. But this isn't a war plant. (*He turns to reassure the others*) Mind you, I don't know if he really knows—or if he doesn't know.

Mr Frank. Offer him half. Then we'll soon find out if it's blackmail or not.

Dussel (*running down* lc) And if it is? We've got to pay it, haven't we? Anything he asks we've got to pay.

Mr Frank (*patiently and calmly*) Let's decide that when the time comes.

(Dussel *moves up* l)

Kraler (*again trying to reassure them*) This may be all my imagination. You get to a point, these days, where you suspect everyone and everything. Again and again—on some simple look or word, I've found myself . . .

Effects Cue 30

(*The telephone rings in the office below*)

Mrs Van Daan (*rising and hurrying to* l *of Kraler; breathless and overwrought*) There's the telephone. What does that mean, the telephone ringing on a holiday?

Kraler. That's my wife. I told her I had to go over some papers in my office—to call me there when she got out of church. (*He rises*) I'll offer him half, then. (*He shakes hands with Mr Frank*) Good-bye—we'll hope for the best.

(Mr Frank *rises. The others half-heartedly call their* "good-byes". Kraler *exits down the stair-well.* Mr Frank *follows him down and bolts the door below.* Mrs Frank *rises to see Kraler out, then sits dispiritedly in the chair above the stair-well. After a moment* Mr Van Daan *slaps his knee in a gesture of resignation, then rises and takes his and Margot's china to the sink.* Mrs Van Daan *crosses above the table and goes into the W.C.*

Lighting Cue 40
The light comes on in the W.C. Peter *puts his cup and plate on the draining-board, then sits above the table*)

Dussel (*to Mr Van Daan*) You can thank your son for this—(*he points to the pendant* c) smashing the light. I tell you, it's just a question of time, now. (*He moves up* c *and stands looking out of the window*)

(Mr Frank *comes up the stair-well*)

Margot. Sometimes I wish the end would come—whatever it is.

Mrs Frank (*rising; shocked*)   Margot!

(Anne *rises, goes to Margot, sits beside her on the couch and puts her arms around her*)

Margot.   Then at least we'd know where we were.

Mrs Frank (*crossing below the table to* RC)   You should be ashamed of yourself. Talking that way. Think how lucky we are. Think of the thousands dying in the war, every day. Think of the people in concentration camps.

Anne (*lashing out at her mother*)   What's the good of that? What's the good of thinking of misery when you're already miserable? That's stupid!

Mrs Frank (*shocked*)   Anne!

(Mr Frank *listens unhappily*)

Anne.   We're young, Margot and Peter and I. (*She rises*) You grown-ups have had your chance. But look at us. If we begin thinking of all the horror in the world, we're lost. We're trying to hold on to some kind of ideals—when everything—ideals, hopes —everything, are being destroyed.

Mrs Frank (*moving to* L *of Anne; trying to get a word in*)   Now, Anne . . .

Anne (*over-riding her*)   It isn't our fault that the world is in such a mess. We weren't around when all this started.

Mrs Frank.   Anne!

Anne.   So don't try to take it out on us. (*She rushes into the room* R, *slams the door after her, picks up a brush from the chest and hurls it to the floor. Then she sits on her bed, trying to control her anger*)

Mr Van Daan (*moving to* R *of Peter*)   She talks as if we started the war. Did we start the war? (*He sees Anne's cake on the table and reaches out to take it*)

(Peter *anticipates Mr Van Daan and picks up the plate*)

Peter.   She left her cake. (*He crosses to the door* R)

(Mr Van Daan *looks after Peter, then turns and goes up the attic stairs, disappearing* R. Mr Frank *gives* Mrs Frank *her cake, and she sits above the table, facing* L *and eating without relish.* Mr Frank *then takes a piece of cake to* Margot *and sits quietly on the couch above her, as she slowly eats.* Peter *goes into the room* R. Anne *sits up quickly, trying to hide the signs of her tears*)

(*He holds out the cake*) You left this.

Anne (*dully*)   Thanks.

(Peter *places the cake on the window-seat, then moves to the door, changes his mind, closes the door and turns to Anne. As he speaks he works back to the window-seat*)

Peter.   I thought you were fine, just now. You know just how

c*

to talk to them. You know just how to say it. I'm no good—I never can think—especially when I'm mad. That Dussel—when he said that about Mouschi—someone eating him—all I could think is—I wanted to hit him. I wanted to give him such a—a—that he'd . . . That's what I used to do when there was an argument at school—that's the way I—but here—and an old man like that—it wouldn't be so good.

ANNE. You're making a big mistake about me. I do it all wrong. I say too much. I go too far. I hurt people's feelings.

(DUSSEL *rises and moves towards the door* R)

PETER. I think you're just fine—what I want to say—if it wasn't for you around here, I don't know. What I mean is . . .

Lighting Cue 41

(DUSSEL *switches on the pendant* R. ANNE *and* PETER *turn to look at him.* DUSSEL *pauses a second, staring back, then moves towards his bed.* PETER *advances towards him, slowly and menacingly.* DUSSEL *retreats, backing out of the door. He looks back forlornly as* PETER *firmly closes the door on him and returns to Anne*)

ANNE. Do you mean it, Peter? Do you really mean it?
PETER. I said it, didn't I?
ANNE. Thank you, Peter.

(DUSSEL, *during the following scene, feeling lost, wanders to the door* L. *After a moment's hesitation he enters the room* L, *sits under the skylight and reads one of Peter's books*)

PETER (*looking at the pictures on the wall*) You've got quite a collection.

ANNE (*rising*) Would you like some in your room? I could give you some. (*She sits on the stool*) Heaven knows you spend enough time in there—doing Heaven knows what.

PETER (*moving to* R *of her*) It's easier. A fight starts, or an argument—I duck in there.

ANNE. You're lucky, having a room to go to. His lordship is always here—I hardly ever get a minute alone. When they start in on me, I can't duck away. I have to stand there and take it.

PETER. You gave some of it back just now.

(MARGOT *cannot finish the cake. She gives it to* MR FRANK, *who rises, places the cake on the table* R, *then helps* MARGOT *lie comfortably again and tucks her in.* MRS FRANK *rises, stacks the china and cutlery from the table and takes it to the sink.* MR FRANK *collects all she cannot manage and takes it to her. She washes as he dries*)

ANNE. I get so mad. They've formed their opinions—about everything—but we—we're still trying to find out. We have problems here that no other people our age have ever had. And just as you think you've solved them, something comes along and bang—you have to start all over again.

PETER. At least you've got someone you can talk to.

ANNE. Not really. Mother—I never discuss anything serious with her. She doesn't understand. Father's all right. We can talk about everything—everything but one thing. Mother. He simply won't talk about her. I don't think you can be really intimate with anyone if he holds something back, do you?

PETER. I think your father's fine.

ANNE. Oh, he is, Peter. He is. He's the only one who's ever given me the feeling that I have any sense. But, anyway, nothing can take the place of school and friends of your own age—or near your age—can it?

PETER. I suppose you miss your friends and all.

ANNE. It isn't just . . . (*She breaks off and stares up at him for a second*) Isn't it funny, you and I? Here we've been seeing each other every minute for almost a year and a half, and this is the first time we've ever really talked. It helps a lot to have someone to talk to, don't you think? It helps you to let off steam.

PETER (*edging to the door*) Well, any time you want to let off steam, you can come into my room.

ANNE (*rising and following him*) I can get up an awful lot of steam. You'll have to be careful how you say that.

PETER. It's all right with me.

ANNE. Do you mean it?

PETER. I said it, didn't I? (*He goes into the centre room*)

(ANNE *stands in her doorway looking after* PETER, *who crosses to the door* L, *stands for a moment looking back at Anne then turns and opens the door.* DUSSEL *rises, passes Peter and goes quickly into the centre room.* ANNE *sees Dussel and quickly shuts the door of the room* R. DUSSEL *turns back towards the room* L. PETER *quickly shuts the door of the room* L. DUSSEL *stands there, bewildered and forlorn.*

Lighting Cue 42

The LIGHTS *fade smoothly except for a spot on Dussel.*

Lighting Cue 43

The spot on Dussel fades. ANNE'S VOICE *is heard in the darkness, faintly at first, then with growing strength*)

ANNE'S VOICE. We've had bad news. The people from whom Miep got our ration books have been arrested. So we have had to cut down on our food. Our stomachs are so empty that they rumble and make strange noises, all in different keys. Mr Van Daan's is deep and low, like a bass fiddle. Mine is high, whistling like a flute. As we all sit around waiting for supper, it's like an orchestra tuning up. It only needs Toscanini to raise his baton and we'd be off in the Ride of the Valkyries. Monday, the sixth of March, nineteen forty-four. Mr Kraler is in the hospital. It seems he has ulcers. Pim says we are his ulcers. Miep has to run the business and us, too. The Americans have landed on the southern tip of Italy. Father looks for a quick finish to the war. Mr Dussel is waiting every day for the warehouse man to demand more money. Have I been skipping too much from one subject to another? I can't help it. I feel that Spring is coming.

Lighting Cue 44

(*The* LIGHTS *come slowly up.* ANNE'S VOICE *starts to fade*)

I feel it in my whole body and soul. I feel utterly confused. I am longing—so longing—for everything—for friends—for someone to talk to—someone who understands—someone young, who feels as I do.

SCENE 2

SCENE—*The same. March 1944. Evening.*

When the LIGHTS *come up, it is after supper.*

Effects Cue 31

Outside we hear the sound of children playing. The grown-ups, with the exception of MR VAN DAAN, *are all in the centre room. He is sitting in the attic room, working on a piece of embroidery in an embroidery frame.* MRS FRANK *is seated in the chair down* L, *mending a glove.* MRS VAN DAAN *is sitting* R *of the table, reading a fashion magazine.* MR FRANK *is sitting on the stool below the table, going over some business ledgers.* DUSSEL *shifts impatiently from foot to foot outside the door of the room* R. *All the lamps are lit.* PETER *is sitting in the room* L, *on the foot of his bed, combing his hair before a small mirror set up on the window-seat. During the ensuing scene, he puts on his tie, polishes his shoes, brushes his coat, puts it on, then makes certain that his room is neat. He is preparing for a visit from Anne. The blackout curtain covers the skylight. A group of photographs is now on the wall* L. *One is slightly tilted.* ANNE *and* MARGOT *are in the room* R. ANNE, *too, is getting dressed. She stands in her slip before the mirror on the dressing-table, putting up her hair.* MARGOT *is seated on Anne's bed, stitching the waistband of a skirt for Anne to wear. The sewing basket is beside her. When the lights are fully up,* DUSSEL *crosses impatiently above the table to* L. *He stops to glance back at the door* R, *then strides down to Mrs Frank and looks at her, appealing for help.* MRS FRANK *becomes more absorbed in her sewing.* DUSSEL *stamps across to the couch.* MRS FRANK *looks unhappily after him.* DUSSEL *sits on the couch, pops up immediately, goes to the door of the room* R *and raps sharply on it.*

ANNE (*calling*)   No, no, Mr Dussel. I am not dressed yet.

(DUSSEL, *furious, moves to the couch, sits on it and buries his head in his hands*)

(*She turns to Margot*) How is that? How does that look?

MARGOT (*glancing briefly at Anne*)   Fine.

ANNE. You didn't even look.

MARGOT. Of course I did. It's fine.

ANNE. Margot, tell me, am I terribly ugly?

(MRS FRANK, *feeling sorry for Dussel, rises and crosses above the table towards the door of the room* R. DUSSEL *half rises and* MRS FRANK *motions him to be patient. He resumes his seat*)

MARGOT. Oh, stop fishing.

ANNE. No. No. Tell me.

MARGOT. Of course you're not. You've got nice eyes—and a lot of animation, and . . .

ANNE (*dryly*) A little vague, aren't you? (*She reaches over, takes a brassière of Margot's out of the sewing basket and tries it on over her slip*)

MRS FRANK (*knocking at the door* R) May I come in?

MARGOT. Come in, Mother.

(MRS FRANK *goes into the room* R *and closes the door behind her*)

MRS FRANK. Mr Dussel's impatient to get in here.

ANNE. Heavens, he takes the room for himself the entire day.

MRS FRANK (*gently*) Anne, dear, you're not going in again tonight to see Peter?

ANNE (*with dignity*) That is my intention. (*She turns to the mirror to study the effect of the brassière*)

MRS FRANK. But you've already spent a great deal of time in there today.

ANNE. I was in there exactly twice. Once to get the dictionary, and then three-quarters of an hour before supper. (*She turns to view herself from another angle*)

MRS FRANK. Aren't you afraid you're disturbing him?

ANNE. Mother, I have some intuition.

MRS FRANK. Then may I ask you this much, Anne. Please don't shut the door when you go in.

ANNE. You sound like Mrs Van Daan. (*She throws the brassière back in the sewing basket, picks up her blouse and puts it on*)

MRS FRANK. No. No. I don't mean to suggest anything wrong. I only wish that you wouldn't expose yourself to criticism—that you wouldn't give Mrs Van Daan the opportunity to be unpleasant.

ANNE. Mrs Van Daan doesn't need an opportunity to be unpleasant.

MRS FRANK. Everyone's on edge, worried about Mr Kraler. This is one more thing . . .

ANNE. I'm sorry, Mother. I'm going to Peter's room. I'm not going to let Petronella Van Daan spoil our friendship.

(MRS FRANK *hesitates a second, then goes into the centre room, closes the door after her, indicates to Dussel that it will not be long now, continues to the shelves up* L, *puts down the glove, gets a pack of cards, then sits* L *of the table and plays solitaire. When Mrs Frank leaves,* ANNE *turns to Margot, indicating she would like to wear her high-heeled shoes.* MARGOT *smiles agreement and* ANNE *hands her a piece of paper from the dressing-table, for Margot to put into the shoes.* MARGOT *gives the skirt to Anne and slips off her shoes*)

MARGOT (*stuffing the paper into the shoes*) Why don't you two talk in the main room? It'd save a lot of trouble. It's hard on mother, having to listen to those remarks from Mrs Van Daan and not say a word.

ANNE (*putting on the skirt*) Why doesn't she say a word? I think it's ridiculous to take it and take it.

MARGOT. You don't understand mother at all, do you? She can't talk back. She's not like you. It's just not in her nature to fight back.

ANNE. Anyway—the only one I worry about is you. I feel awfully guilty about you. (*She sits on the stool, putting on Margot's high-heeled shoes*)

MARGOT. What about?

ANNE. I mean, every time I go into Peter's room, I have a feeling I may be hurting you.

    (MARGOT *shakes her head*)

(*She rises then sits on the foot of the bed with Margot*) I know if it were me, I'd be wild. I'd be desperately jealous, if it were me.

MARGOT. Well, I'm not.

ANNE. You don't feel badly? Really? Truly? You're not jealous?

MARGOT. Of course I'm jealous—jealous that you've got something to get up in the morning for—but jealous of you and Peter? No.

ANNE (*rising and moving to the mirror*) Maybe there's nothing to be jealous of. Maybe he doesn't really like me. Maybe I'm just taking the place of his cat. (*She picks up a pair of short white gloves and puts them on*) Wouldn't you like to come in with us?

MARGOT. I have a book.

    (DUSSEL *can stand it no longer. He jumps up, goes to the door* R *and knocks sharply*)

DUSSEL. Will you please let me in my room.

ANNE. Just a minute, dear, dear Mr Dussel. (*She picks up her mother's pink shawl, adjusts it elegantly over her shoulders, gives a last look in the mirror, then goes to the door* R *and turns to Margot*)

    (MARGOT *rises and moves to Anne*)

Well, here I go—to run the gauntlet. (*She goes into the centre room*)

Lighting Cue 45

(MARGOT *switches off the pendant* R *and goes into the centre room*)

DUSSEL (*sarcastically*)   Thank you so much.

(ANNE *gives* DUSSEL *a dignified bow. He goes into the room* R *and closes the door.* ANNE *crosses below the table, trying to appear very sophisticated*)

MRS VAN DAAN.   My God, look at her!

(ANNE *pays no attention and continues towards the room* L. *Margot's heels give her a bit of trouble, but her head is high.* DUSSEL *takes a pair of trousers from a hook down* R, *scissors from the chest of drawers, sits on his bed and trims the frayed turn-ups.* MARGOT *takes her sewing basket, puts it on the shelves up* L, *gets her crossword puzzle book and pencil, crosses to the couch, adjusts the lamp, then sits on the couch and fills in a puzzle.* ANNE *knocks at the door* L. PETER *makes a quick check to see all is in order*)

I don't know what good it is to have a son. I never see him. He wouldn't care if I killed myself.

(PETER *opens the door and stands aside for Anne to enter*)

(*She rises*) Just a minute, Anne. (*She crosses above the table to Anne*) I'd like to say a few words to my son. Do you mind? Peter, I don't want you staying up till all hours tonight. You've got to have your sleep. You're a growing boy. You hear?

MRS FRANK.   Anne won't stay late. She's going to bed promptly at nine. Aren't you, Anne?

ANNE.   Yes, Mother. (*To Mrs Van Daan. Too sweetly*) May we go now?

Effects Cue 31a

(*The sound of the children playing outside fades*)

MRS VAN DAAN.   Are you asking me? I didn't know I had anything to say about it.

MRS FRANK.   Listen for the chimes, Anne dear.

(PETER *and* ANNE *go into the room* L *and close the door*)

MRS VAN DAAN (*moving to* L *of Mrs Frank*)   In my day it was the boys who called on the girls.

MRS FRANK.   You know how young people like to feel that they have secrets. Peter's room is the only place where they can talk.

Lighting Cue 46

(*The light very slowly fades as twilight falls*)

MRS VAN DAAN.   Talk! That's not what they called it when I was young. (*She crosses to the fireplace, puts her magazine on the mantelpiece, goes to the sink, picks up her apron, puts it on, then polishes the coffee-pot*)

ANNE (*turning indignantly to Peter*) Aren't they awful? Aren't they impossible? Treating us as if we're still in the nursery.

PETER. Don't let it bother you. It doesn't bother me.

ANNE. I suppose you can't really blame them—(*she sits on the foot of Peter's bed, facing front*) they think back to what they were like at our age. They don't realize how much more advanced we are. When I think what wonderful discussions we've had . . . Oh, I forgot. I was going to bring you some more pictures.

(PETER *takes out a bottle of orange squash and two glasses from his box-table*)

PETER. Oh, these are fine, thanks.

ANNE. Don't you want some more? Miep just brought me some new ones.

PETER. Maybe later. (*He sits on the window-seat, facing* ANNE, *hands her a glass, pours some orange into it, then takes some for himself*)

Lighting Cue 47

(MRS VAN DAAN *puts down the coffee-pot, goes into the W.C. and turns on the light*)

ANNE (*looking at one of the photographs*) I remember when I got that—I won it. I bet Jopie that I could eat five ice cream cones. We'd all been playing ping-pong. We used to have heavenly times—we'd finish up with ice cream at the *Delphi*, or the *Oasis*, where Jews were allowed. There'd always be a lot of boys—we'd laugh and joke. I'd like to go back to it for a few days or a week. But after that I know I'd be bored to death. I think more seriously about life, now. I want to be a journalist—or something. I love to write. What do you want to do?

(MR FRANK *rises, picks up his ledgers and moves* R. MARGOT *stops him and asks for help on a word. He cannot make a suggestion and continues to the shelves up* L, *puts down the books and gets a small chess set. He circles and sits below the table where he and* MRS FRANK *play chess*)

PETER. I thought I might go off some place—work on a farm or something—some job that doesn't take much brains.

ANNE. You shouldn't talk that way. You've got the most awful inferiority complex.

PETER. I know I'm not smart.

ANNE. That isn't true. You're much better than I am in dozens of things—arithmetic and algebra and . . . Well, you're a million times better than I am in algebra. (*With sudden directness*) You like Margot, don't you? Right from the start you liked her, liked her much better than me.

PETER (*uncomfortably*) Oh, I don't know.

(DUSSEL *replaces the trousers on the hook, gets a nail file from the dressing-table, sits on the bed and files his nails*)

ANNE. It's all right. Everyone feels that way. Margot's so good. She's sweet and bright and beautiful, and I'm not.

PETER. I wouldn't say that.

ANNE. Oh, no, I'm not. I know that. I know quite well that I'm not a beauty. I never have been and never shall be.

PETER. I don't agree at all. I think you're pretty.

ANNE. That's not true.

PETER. And another thing. You've changed—from at first, I mean.

ANNE. I have?

PETER. I used to think you were awful noisy.

ANNE (eagerly) And what do you think now, Peter? How have I changed?

PETER. Well—er—you're—quieter.

ANNE (amused) I'm glad you don't just hate me.

PETER. I never said that.

ANNE. I bet when you get out of here you'll never think of me again.

PETER. That's crazy.

ANNE. When you get back with all of your friends, you're going to say—"now what did I ever see in that Mrs Quack Quack?"

PETER. I haven't got any friends.

ANNE. Oh, Peter, of course you have. Everyone has friends.

PETER. Not me. I don't want any. I get along all right without them.

ANNE. Does that mean you can get along without me? I think of myself as your friend.

PETER. No. If they were all like you, it'd be different. (He realizes what he has said. To cover his embarrassment he hurriedly picks up the glasses and bottle and returns them to the box-table)

(There is a second's silence and then ANNE speaks, hesitantly and shyly. She cannot look at Peter)

ANNE. Peter, did you ever kiss a girl?

PETER. Yes. Once.

(ANNE looks quickly back over her shoulder at him)

ANNE (to cover her feelings) That picture's crooked. (She looks away)

(PETER straightens the picture)

Was she pretty?

PETER. Huh?

ANNE. The girl that you kissed.

PETER. I don't know. I was blindfolded. (He resumes his place opposite her) It was at a party. One of those kissing games.

Lighting Cue 48

(MRS VAN DAAN *turns off the W.C. light, comes into the centre room, goes to the sink and polishes the coffee-pot*)

ANNE (*relieved*) Oh, I don't suppose that really counts, does it?
PETER. It didn't with me.

(DUSSEL *rises, puts down the nail file, picks up his pyjamas and comes into the centre room*)

ANNE. I've been kissed twice. Once a man I'd never seen before kissed me on the cheek when he picked me up off the ice and I was crying. And the other was Mr Koophuis, a friend of father's who kissed my hand. You wouldn't say those counted, would you?
PETER. I wouldn't say so.
ANNE. I know almost for certain that Margot would never kiss anyone unless she was engaged to them. And I'm sure, too, that mother never touched a man before Pim.

Lighting Cue 49

(DUSSEL *goes into the W.C. and turns on the light*)

But I don't know—things are so different now. What do you think? Do you think a girl shouldn't kiss anyone except if she's engaged or something? It's so hard to try to think what to do, when here we are with the whole world falling around our ears and you think—well—you don't know what's going to happen tomorrow, and . . . What do you think?
PETER. I suppose it'd depend on the girl. Some girls, anything they do's wrong. But others—well—it wouldn't necessarily be wrong with them.

Effects Cue 32

(*The carillon chimes and strikes nine o'clock*)

I've always thought that when two people . . .
ANNE. Nine o'clock. I have to go.
PETER. That's right.
ANNE (*without moving*) Good night.

(*Their faces are close together. There is a second's pause, then* PETER, *too shy to kiss Anne, rises and moves away*)

PETER. You won't let them stop you coming?
ANNE. No. (*She rises, moves to the door and turns*) Some time I might bring my diary. There are so many things in it that I want to talk over with you. There's a lot about you.
PETER. What kind of things?
ANNE. I wouldn't want you to see some of it. I thought you were a nothing, just the way you thought about me.
PETER. Did you change your mind, the way I changed my mind about you?
ANNE. Well—you'll see . . .

(*For a second* Anne *stands looking up at* Peter, *longing for him to kiss her. As he makes no move, she turns to go. Then suddenly he grabs her and, turning her around, holds her awkwardly in his arms, kissing her on the cheek.* Anne, *dazed, floats slowly out of the room. She stands for a minute, her back to the people in the centre room, shutting the door of the room* L *behind her. After a moment her poise returns, and with a sophisticated motion she flips one end of her shawl back over her shoulder. Then she goes to Mr and Mrs Frank and silently kisses them good night.* Mr *and* Mrs Frank *murmur their "good nights".* Anne *crosses to Margot, kisses her, then goes to the door* R. Mr *and* Mrs Frank *stop their game and watch Anne.* Anne *is suddenly aware of Mrs Van Daan at the sink, goes quickly to her, takes Mrs Van Daan's face in her hands and kisses her first on one cheek and then on the other, then goes into the room* R *and closes the door.* Mrs Van Daan *moves slowly above the table and watches Anne go, then looks slowly across towards the room* L. *Her suspicions are confirmed.* Mr *and* Mrs Frank *return to their game*)

Mrs Van Daan (*knowingly*)   Ah, hah! (*She shakes her head*)

Lighting Cue 50

(*The* Lights *fade swiftly. We hear* Anne's Voice *in the darkness, faintly, at first, then with growing strength*)

Anne's Voice. By this time we all know each other so well that if anyone starts to tell a story, the rest can finish it for him. We're having to cut down still further on our meals. What makes it worse, the rats have been at work again. They've carried off some of our precious food. Even Mr Dussel wishes now that Mouschi was here. Thursday, the twentieth of April, nineteen forty-four. Invasion fever is mounting every day. Miep tells us that people outside talk of nothing else. For myself, life has become much more pleasant. I often go to Peter's room after supper. Oh, don't think I'm in love, because I'm not. But it does make life more bearable to have someone with whom you can exchange views. No more tonight. P.S. I must be honest. I must confess that I actually live for the next meeting. Is there anything lovelier than to sit under the skylight and feel the sun on your cheeks and have a darling boy in your arms? I admit now that I'm glad the Van Daans had a son and not a daughter.

Lighting Cue 51

(*The* Lights *come slowly up.* Anne's Voice *fades out*)

I've outgrown another dress. That's the third. I'm having to wear Margot's clothes after all. I'm working hard on my French —and am now reading *La Belle Nivernaise.*

SCENE 3

SCENE—*The same. April 1944. Night.*

When the LIGHTS *come up, everyone is in bed and all is quiet. A dim cool light falls through the skylight in the room* L. *The back-cloth is slightly illuminated. We can faintly see* MR *and* MRS FRANK *and* ANNE *in their beds.* MARGOT *sleeps up* L *behind the drawn curtain. Suddenly in the attic room a match flares up for a moment and then is quickly put out.* MR VAN DAAN, *in bare feet, dressed in underwear and trousers, is dimly seen coming stealthily down the attic stairs and into the centre room. He goes to the food cupboard under the sink and again lights a match. Then he cautiously opens the cupboard and takes out a half loaf of bread. As he closes the cupboard, it creaks. He stands rigid.* MRS FRANK *sits up in bed and sees Mr Van Daan.*

MRS FRANK (*screaming*) Otto! Otto! Come quick.

(*The others wake and hurriedly get up*)

MR FRANK. What is it? What's happened?

(MR VAN DAAN *starts for the stairs, becomes confused and continues across up* L. MARGOT *hurriedly gets the stool from above the sofa and drags it under the pendant* C)

MRS FRANK (*rushing to Mr Van Daan*) He's stealing the food.

(DUSSEL *dashes out of the room* R *towards Mr Van Daan.* ANNE *follows, after throwing a skirt over her shoulders like a shawl*)

DUSSEL. You! You! Give me that.

(PETER *comes out of the room* L)

MRS VAN DAAN (*getting out of bed*) Putti—Putti—what is it?

(*The following speeches overlap*)

DUSSEL (*grabbing the bread*) You dirty thief——

(MR VAN DAAN *backs down* L)

—stealing food—you good-for-nothing . . .

Lighting Cue 52

(MARGOT *switches on the pendant* C)

MR FRANK (*putting his arms round Dussel's waist and tugging*) Mr Dussel. For God's sake! Help me, Peter.

(PETER *works down behind his father and pulls at his shoulders*)

PETER (*to Dussel*) Let him go. Let go.

(DUSSEL *and* MR FRANK *give a tug that pulls* MR VAN DAAN *to his knees.* DUSSEL *has the bread.* MR VAN DAAN *rises quickly and retreats down* RC)

DUSSEL. You greedy, selfish . . .

MRS VAN DAAN (*coming down the attic stairs*) Putti—what is it?

(*All of* MRS FRANK's *gentleness, her self-control is gone. She is outraged, in a frenzy of indignation*)

MRS FRANK. The bread! He was stealing the bread.

(DUSSEL *stands above the left end of the table and places the bread on it.* PETER, *humiliated, sits on the stairs* L)

DUSSEL. It was you, and all the time we thought it was the rats.

MR FRANK. Mr Van Daan, how could you!

MR VAN DAAN (*facing* R) I'm hungry.

(DUSSEL *crosses, goes into the room* R, *puts on his suit jacket, then returns and sits in the chair above the stair-well.* MRS VAN DAAN *moves protectively around the right end of the table to Mr Van Daan and stands* L *of him*)

MRS FRANK (*with righteous rage*) We're all of us hungry. I see the children getting thinner and thinner. Your own son Peter—I've heard him moan in his sleep, he's so hungry. (*She moves around the left end of the table and stands below it*) And you come in the night and steal food that should go to them—to the children.

MRS VAN DAAN. He needs more food than the rest of us. He's used to more. He's a big man.

(MR VAN DAAN *moves to the fireplace*)

MRS FRANK (*turning on Mrs Van Daan*) And you—you're worse than he is. You're a mother, and yet you sacrifice your child to this man—this—this . . . (*She moves above the table*)

MR FRANK (*moving to* L *of Mrs Frank*) Edith! Edith!

(MARGOT *picks up the shawl from the chair* R *of the table and puts it over Mrs Frank's shoulders*)

MRS FRANK (*paying no attention; to Mrs Van Daan*) Don't think I haven't seen you. Always saving the choicest bits for him. I've watched you day after day and I've held my tongue. But not any longer. Not after this. Now, I want him to go. I want him to get out of here. (*She moves up* C)

MR FRANK   } (*together*) { Edith!
MR VAN DAAN   }   { Get out of here?

MRS VAN DAAN (*sinking into the chair* R *of the table*) What do you mean?

MRS FRANK. Just that. Take your things and get out.

(MR VAN DAAN *sits on the upstage end of the couch*)

MR FRANK (*to his wife*) You're speaking in anger. You cannot mean what you are saying.

MRS FRANK. I mean exactly that.

D

MR FRANK. For two long years we have lived here, side by side. We have respected each other's rights—we have managed to live in peace. Are we now going to throw it all away? (*He crosses and stands above the right end of the table*)

(MR VAN DAAN *becomes ill, fears that he is going to retch and rises*)

I know this will never happen again, will it, Mr Van Daan?

MR VAN DAAN. No, no. (*Holding his mouth and stomach, he moves towards the W.C.*)

(ANNE *puts her arms around* MR VAN DAAN *and helps him up the steps*

Lighting Cue 53

MR VAN DAAN *goes into the W.C. and switches on the light.* MRS VAN DAAN *rises to help, but they have gone. She moves to the couch, takes a cover from the bed and puts it around her shoulders*)

MRS FRANK. He steals once! He'll steal again.

MR FRANK. Edith, please! Let us be calm. We'll all go to our rooms—and afterwards we'll sit down quietly and talk this out —we'll find some way . . .

MRS FRANK. No! No! No more talk. I want them to leave.

(MR FRANK *realizes he cannot reason with his wife, makes a hopeless gesture and goes to Anne and Margot up* RC)

MRS VAN DAAN (*wandering below the table to* L) You'd put us out, on the streets?

MRS FRANK. There are other hiding places.

MRS VAN DAAN. A cellar—a closet. I know. And we have no money left even to pay for that.

MRS FRANK. I'll give you money. Out of my own pocket I'll give it gladly. (*She gets her purse from the shelves up* L *and returns with it to the table* C)

(MR FRANK *moves and stands above the right end of the table*)

MRS VAN DAAN (*moving above the left end of the table*) Mr Frank, you told Putti you'd never forget what he'd done for you when you came to Amsterdam. You said you could never repay him, that you . . .

MRS FRANK (*counting out money*) If my husband had any obligation to you, he's paid it, over and over.

MR FRANK. Edith, I've never seen you like this before. I don't know you.

MRS FRANK. I should have spoken out long ago.

DUSSEL. You can't be nice to some people.

MRS VAN DAAN (*to Dussel*) There would have been plenty for all of us, if *you* hadn't come in here.

MR FRANK. We don't need the Nazis to destroy us. We're

destroying ourselves. (*He sits* R *of the table, with his head in his hands*)

MRS FRANK (*turning to Mrs Van Daan*) Give this to Miep. She'll find you a place. (*She forces the money into Mrs Van Daan's hand and returns her purse to the shelves up* L)

ANNE (*crossing to Mrs Frank*) Mother, you're not putting *Peter* out. Peter hasn't done anything.

MRS FRANK. He'll stay, of course. When I say the children, I mean Peter, too.

PETER (*rising*) I'd have to go if father goes.

Lighting Cue 54

(MR VAN DAAN *switches out the W.C. light and comes into the centre room.* MRS VAN DAAN *hurries to him and takes him to the couch where he sits on the upstage end, then she goes to the sink, gets some water and bathes her husband's face*)

MRS FRANK (*standing above the table; to Peter*) He's no father to you—that man. He doesn't know what it is to be a father.

PETER (*turning towards the room* L) I wouldn't feel right. I couldn't stay.

MRS FRANK (*moving up* C) Very well, then. I'm sorry.

ANNE (*rushing to Peter*) No, Peter! No!

(PETER *goes into the room* L, *closes the door and goes into his closet area*)

(*She turns to her mother, crying*) I don't care about the food. They can have mine. I don't want it. Only don't send them away. It'll be daylight soon. They'll be caught.

MARGOT. Please, Mother!

MRS FRANK. They're not going now. They'll stay here until Miep finds them a hiding place. (*She stands above the table. To Mrs Van Daan*) But one thing I insist on. He must never come down here again. He must never come to this room where the food is stored. We'll divide what we have—an equal share for each.

(DUSSEL *rises, crosses to the cupboard under the sink and takes a bag of potatoes from it*)

You can cook it here and take it up to him. (*She moves up* C)

(DUSSEL *puts the potatoes on the table*)

MARGOT (*moving to* L *of Dussel*) Oh, no! No. We haven't sunk so far that we're going to fight over a handful of rotten potatoes.

DUSSEL (*dividing the potatoes into piles*) Mrs Frank—Mr Frank—Margot—Anne—Peter—Mrs Van Daan—Mr Van Daan—myself—Mrs Frank . . .

Effects Cue 33

(*The buzzer sounds Miep's signal. All freeze for an instant*)

MR FRANK (*rising quickly*) It's Miep. (*He hurries to the couch, snatches up his overcoat, puts it on and crosses to the stair-well*)

MARGOT. At this hour?

(MR VAN DAAN *rises and moves down* R)

MRS FRANK (*moving down* R *of the table*) It must be trouble.

MR FRANK (*stopping and turning; to Dussel*) I beg you, don't let her see a thing like this.

DUSSEL (*who has been counting without stopping*) Anne—Peter—Mrs Van Daan—Mr Van Daan—myself—Mrs Frank . . .

MARGOT (*to Dussel; overlapping*) Stop it! Stop it!

(MR FRANK *goes down the stair-well and opens the door*)

DUSSELL. Mr Frank—Margot—Anne—Peter—Mrs Van Daan—Mr Van Daan—myself—Mrs Frank . . .

MRS VAN DAAN (*pointing at the potato piles*) You're keeping the big ones for yourself. (*She crosses and stands below the table*) All the big ones—look at the size of that—and that . . .

(DUSSEL *continues with his dividing.* PETER, *with his shirt and trousers on, comes from the room* L *and stops just outside the door*)

MARGOT (*to Dussel*) Stop it! Stop it!

MIEP (*off; excitedly*) Mr Frank—the most wonderful news—the invasion has begun.

MR FRANK (*off*) No! No!

(MIEP *runs up the stair-well, ahead of* MR FRANK. *She has a man's raincoat over her nightclothes, and carries a bunch of flowers*)

MIEP. Did you hear that everybody? Did you hear what I said? The invasion has begun.

(*They all stare at Miep, unable to grasp what she is telling them.* MR FRANK *comes up the stair-well and stands down* L)

The invasion!

(PETER *is the first to recover his wits*)

PETER. Where?

MIEP. It began early this morning.

(*As Miep speaks, the others, all except* MR VAN DAAN, *crowd around her, listening tensely*)

MRS FRANK. How do you know?

MIEP. The radio. The B.B.C. They said they landed on the coast of Normandy.

PETER. The British?

MIEP. British, Americans, French, Dutch, Poles, Norwegians—all of them. More than four thousand ships.

(*As Miep goes on, the realization of what is happening begins to come to them, and everyone goes crazy with excitement*)

Churchill spoke, and General Eisenhower. "D-Day", they call it.

(*A wild demonstration takes place.* PETER *rushes to the kitchen area and grabs a frying pan.* ANNE *follows him.* PETER *starts to march around the room, followed by* ANNE, *and then by* MARGOT. *They circle the table, singing the Dutch National Anthem. They dum-ta-dum the melody, not using the words.* MIEP *gives Margot the bunch of flowers as Margot passes her.* PETER *pounds out the beat of the music on the frying pan.* PETER *and* ANNE *end up* R, *inspecting the map hanging above the mantelpiece.* MARGOT *distributes flowers to everyone. During this the grown-ups embrace each other. All enmities are forgotten in the exhilaration of the wonderful news.* MRS FRANK *hugs Mr Van Daan, as* MR FRANK *hugs Miep and Mrs Van Daan*)

MR FRANK. Thank God it's come.
MRS VAN DAAN. At last.

(MRS FRANK *turns from Mr Van Daan to go to Miep and Mr Frank. Only* MR VAN DAAN *does not join in the excitement. He is too ashamed of himself.* MRS FRANK *meets Mrs Van Daan down* C *as* MRS VAN DAAN *is going over to embrace her husband. The two women hug each other with warm affection, then* MRS FRANK *hugs Miep and Mr Frank.* MRS VAN DAAN *gives her husband an ecstatic embrace, then moves to Dussel.* MR VAN DAAN *sits on the downstage end of the couch, too heartbroken to rejoice with the rest. As* MRS VAN DAAN *goes up to hug* DUSSEL, MRS FRANK *has the same thought and the two women do a little dance of jubilation with him, then* MRS FRANK *hurries down* L *as* MIEP *moves towards the stair-well*)

MIEP (*at the stair-well*) I'm going to tell Mr Kraler—this'll be better than any blood transfusion.
MR FRANK (*stopping Miep*) What part of Normandy did they land, did they say?
MIEP. Normandy—that's all I know now. I'll be up the minute I hear some more.

(MIEP *exits quickly down the stair-well*)

MR FRANK (*taking his wife in his arms*) What did I tell you! What did I tell you!

(MRS FRANK *indicates that* MR FRANK *has forgotten to bolt the door after Miep, and he hurries down the stair-well.* MARGOT *goes down* R *to give a flower to* MR VAN DAAN. *As she holds it out to him, he suddenly breaks into a convulsive sob.* MRS VAN DAAN *rushes to her husband and sits above him on the couch, trying to comfort him.* MARGOT, *not understanding the outburst, retreats below the table*)

MRS VAN DAAN. Putti! Putti! What is it? What happened?
MR VAN DAAN. Please. I'm so ashamed.

(MR FRANK *comes up the stair-well*)

DUSSEL (*moving down* LC; *impatiently*) Oh, for God's sake . . .
(*He goes to the table and replaces the potatoes in the bag*)
MRS VAN DAAN (*comfortingly*) Don't, Putti.
MARGOT. It doesn't matter, now.
MR FRANK (*crossing to Mr Van Daan*) Didn't you hear what
Miep said? The invasion has come. We're going to be liberated.
This is a time to celebrate. (*He hurries up* C *and gets the cognac and a
glass, which he brings to the table, where he pours a stiff drink*)
MR VAN DAAN. To steal bread from children.
MRS FRANK (*moving below the left end of the table*) We've all done
things that we're ashamed of.
ANNE (*moving to Mrs Van Daan*) Look at me, the way I've
treated mother—so mean and horrid to her.
MRS FRANK. No, Anneline, no.
ANNE (*moving to Mrs Frank and putting her arms around her*) Oh,
Mother, I was. I was awful.

(DUSSEL, *the bag of potatoes under his arm and the flower in his
hand, circles* L *of the table*)

MR VAN DAAN. Not like me. No-one is as bad as me.
DUSSEL (*crossing below the table to Mr Van Daan*) Stop it now!
Let's be happy.
MR FRANK (*giving the glass of cognac to Mr Van Daan*) Here!
Here! Schnapps! L'chaim!

(MR VAN DAAN *takes the cognac. They all watch him.* ANNE *puts
up her fingers in a V-for-Victory sign. As* MR VAN DAAN *gives a
faint smile and an answering V-sign, they are startled to hear a loud
wailing sob from behind them. They all look over to* MRS FRANK *who,
stricken with remorse, sinks into the chair down* L *and wails*)

(*He crosses to Mrs Frank*) Edith . . . (*He pats her hand*)

(ANNE *and* MARGOT *rush across, kneel at Mrs Frank's feet and
comfort her*)

MRS FRANK (*through her sobs*) When I think of the terrible
things I said . . .

(MR VAN DAAN *rises, crosses to Mrs Frank and makes a V-sign*)

MR VAN DAAN (*earnestly*) No! No! You were right.
MRS FRANK (*still sobbing*) That I should speak that way to you
—our friends—our guests . . .
DUSSEL. Stop it! You're spoiling——

Lighting Cue 55

(*The scene lights quickly dim out, leaving the group lit by a spot*)
—the whole invasion.

Lighting Cue 56

(*The spot dims swiftly out.* ANNE'S VOICE *is heard faintly at first, and then with growing strength*)

ANNE'S VOICE. We're all in much better spirits these days. There's still excellent news of the invasion. The best part about it is that I have a feeling that friends are coming. Who knows? Maybe I'll be back in school by Autumn. Ha, ha! The joke is on us. The warehouse man doesn't know a thing and we are paying him all that money. Wednesday, the second of July, nineteen forty-four. The invasion seems temporarily to be bogged down. Mr Kraler has to have an operation, which looks bad. The Gestapo have found the radio that was stolen. Mr Dussel says they'll trace it back and back to the thief, and then, it's just a matter of time till they get to us. Everyone is low. Even poor Pim can't raise their spirits. I have often been downcast myself— but never in despair. I can shake off everything if I write. But— and that is the great question—will I ever be able to write well? I want to so much. I want to go on living even after my death.

Lighting Cue 57

(*The* LIGHTS *come slowly up and* ANNE'S VOICE *fades*)

Another birthday has gone by, so now I am fifteen. Already I know what I want. I have a goal, an opinion.

SCENE 4

SCENE—*The same. July 1944. Afternoon.*

When the LIGHTS *come up, everyone but Margot is in the centre room. There is a sense of great tension.*

Effects Cue 34

In the distance a German military band is heard in a rendition of some Viennese waltzes. DUSSEL *is standing at the window up* C, *looking down fixedly at the street below.* MARGOT *is at the dressing-table in the room* R. *The table-lamp* R *is on.* PETER *is sitting* L *of the table, with his copybooks, trying to do his lessons.* ANNE *sits* R *of the table, writing in her diary.* MRS VAN DAAN *is seated on the couch, a book beside her, her eyes on* MR FRANK *as he sits in the chair down* L. MRS FRANK *is up* C, *looking fearfully towards the stair-well.* MR VAN DAAN *is pacing from* C *to* R. *He reverses and goes to Mr Frank. There is no reaction from* MR FRANK *so* MR VAN DAAN *paces* R *again and is down* RC *when the telephone in the office below begins to ring.*

Effects Cue 35

MR VAN DAAN *turns and looks towards the stair-well.* MRS FRANK *stands rigid, tight with fear. They all freeze and listen intently.* DUSSEL *rushes down* L *of the table to Mr Frank. The telephone continues to ring.*

DUSSEL. There it goes again, the telephone. Mr Frank, do you hear?

MR FRANK (*quietly*) Yes. I hear.

DUSSEL (*pleading and insistent*) But this is the third time, Mr Frank. The third time in quick succession. It's a signal. I tell you it's Miep, trying to warn us. For some reason she can't come to us and she's trying to warn us of something.

MR FRANK. Please. Please.

MR VAN DAAN (*moving up* R *of the table; to Dussel*) You're wasting your breath.

DUSSEL. Something has happened, Mr Frank. For three days now Miep hasn't been to see us. And today not a man has come to work. There hasn't been a sound in the building.

MRS FRANK. Perhaps it's Sunday. We may have lost track of the days.

MR VAN DAAN (*to Anne*) You with the diary there. What day is it?

(ANNE *closes the diary so he cannot read what she is writing*)

DUSSEL (*moving to* L *of Mrs Frank*) I don't lose track of the days. I know exactly what day it is. It's Friday, the fourth of August. Friday, and not a man at work. (*He rushes down to Mr Frank, pleading with him, almost in tears*) I tell you Mr Kraler's dead. That's the only explanation. He's dead and they've closed down the building, and Miep's trying to tell us.

MR FRANK. She'd never telephone us.

DUSSEL (*indicating the ringing telephone; frantically*) Mr Frank, answer that. I beg you, answer it.

MR FRANK. No.

MR VAN DAAN (*hurrying around the right end of the table and crossing to Mr Frank*) Just pick it up and listen. You don't have to speak. Just listen and see if it's Miep.

DUSSEL. For God's sake—I ask you.

MR FRANK (*firmly*) No. I've told you "no". I'll do nothing that might let anyone know we're in the building.

PETER. Mr Frank's right.

MR VAN DAAN (*wheeling on his son*) There's no need to tell us what side you're on.

MR FRANK. If we wait patiently, quietly, I believe that help will come.

(*There is silence for a minute as they all listen to the telephone ringing.* DUSSEL *moves up* C. MR VAN DAAN *circles* R *of the table and stands above it*)

DUSSEL. I'm going down. (*He rushes down the stair-well*)

(MR FRANK *rises and tries ineffectually to stop him.*

Effects Cue 35a

When DUSSEL *reaches the outside door, the telephone stops, but he rushes out anyway.* MR FRANK *waits tensely, wondering if he should go after Dussel.* MRS FRANK *moves to the stair-well and gazes tensely down.* PETER *rises. After a moment* DUSSEL *returns, shuts the door and comes up the stairs)*

Too late.

(MR FRANK *crosses above the table and goes into the room* R. *He looks out of the edge of the blackout curtain, then goes to Margot.* DUSSEL *goes to the window up* C. MRS FRANK *goes to the sink, gets some potatoes and a knife, sits on the padded stool above the stove and peels the potatoes)*

MR VAN DAAN. So we just wait here until we die.

MRS VAN DAAN (*hysterically*) I can't stand it! I'll kill myself. I'll kill myself.

MR VAN DAAN (*moving below the table*) For God's sake, stop it!

MRS VAN DAAN. I think you'd be glad if I did. I think you want me to die.

MR VAN DAAN (*crossing to Mrs Van Daan*) Whose fault is it we're here?

(MRS VAN DAAN *covers her ears*)

We could've been safe somewhere—in America or Switzerland.

(MRS VAN DAAN *rises and crosses to the attic stairs*)

(*He follows Mrs Van Daan, shouting*) But no! No! You wouldn't leave when I wanted to. You couldn't leave your things. You couldn't leave your precious furniture. (*He grabs her arm*)

MRS VAN DAAN (*shaking him off*) Don't touch me! (*She goes quickly up to the attic room*)

(MR VAN DAAN *follows slowly after her.* PETER, *humiliated and desperate, goes into the room* L. ANNE, *deeply concerned, looks after him.* PETER *throws himself face down on his bed.* MRS VAN DAAN, *sobbing quietly, lies on her bed.* MR FRANK *comes into the centre room, goes to the couch, sits, picks up a book and tries to read.* ANNE *rises and goes quietly into the room* L, *closing the door behind her. She sits on the edge of the bed, leans over Peter, holds him in her arms and tries to bring him out of his despair.* PETER *is too unhappy to respond*)

ANNE (*after a pause; looking up through the skylight*) Look, Peter, the sky. What a lovely day. Aren't the clouds beautiful? You know what I do when it seems as if I couldn't stand being cooped up for one more minute? I *think* myself out. I think myself on a walk in the park where I used to go with Pim. Where the daffodils and the crocus and the violets grow down the slopes. You know the most wonderful thing about *thinking* yourself out? You can have it any way you like. You can have roses and violets and chrysanthemums all blooming at the same time. It's funny—I used to take it all for granted—and now I've gone crazy about everything to do with nature. Haven't you?

PETER (*barely lifting his face*) I've just gone crazy. I think if something doesn't happen soon—if we don't get out of here . . . I can't stand much more of it.

ANNE (*softly*) I wish you had a religion, Peter.

PETER (*rolling over; bitterly*) No, thanks. Not me.

ANNE. Oh, I don't mean you have to be Orthodox—or believe in heaven and hell and purgatory and things—I just mean some religion—it doesn't matter what. Just to believe in something. When I think of all that's out there—the trees—and flowers—and seagulls—when I think of the dearness of you, Peter—and the goodness of the people we know—Mr Kraler, Miep, Dirk, the vegetable man, all risking their lives for us every day—when I think of these good things, I'm not afraid any more—I find myself, and God, and I . . .

PETER (*rising; impatiently*) That's fine! But when I begin to think, I get mad. Look at us, hiding out for two years. Not able to move. Caught here like . . . Waiting for them to come and get us—and all for what?

ANNE (*rising*) We're not the only people that've had to suffer. There've always been people that've had to—sometimes one race—sometimes another—and yet . . .

PETER (*sitting on the upstage end of his bed*) That doesn't make me feel any better.

ANNE. I know it's terrible, trying to have any faith—when people are doing such horrible . . . (*She gently lifts his face*) But you know what I sometimes think? I think the world may be going through a phase, the way I was with mother. It'll pass, maybe not for hundreds of years, but some day. I still believe, in spite of everything, that people are really good at heart.

PETER (*rising and moving to the window-seat*) I want to see something now—not a thousand years from now.

ANNE (*moving to him*) But, Peter, if you'd only look at it as part of a great pattern—that we're just a little minute in life . . . (*She breaks off, with a rueful smile*) Listen to us, going at each other like a couple of stupid grown-ups. (*She holds out her hand to him*)

(PETER *takes Anne's hand*)

Look at the sky, now. Isn't it lovely?

(PETER *stands behind Anne with his arms around her. They look up at the sky*)

Some day, when we're outside again, I'm going to . . .

Effects Cue 36

(ANNE *breaks off as she hears the sound of a car outside, its brakes*

*squealing as it comes to a sudden stop. The people in the other rooms
also become aware of the sound, and all listen tensely.*

Effects Cue 37

Another car outside roars up to a sudden stop. Mr Frank, *book
in hand, rises slowly. Everyone is listening, hardly breathing.*

Effects Cue 38

Suddenly a heavy electric bell begins clanging savagely below.
Anne *and* Peter *hurry from the room* L. *She stops just outside the
door. He remains on the first step.* Margot *hurries into the centre
room.*

Mrs Frank *puts down the potatoes and stands above the chair*
R *of the table.* Mrs Van Daan *rises and comes fearfully down the
attic stairs.* Mr Van Daan *stays above at the head of the staircase. All
eyes are fixed on* Mr Frank, *who crosses slowly and calmly towards
the stair-well. He drops the book on the chair down* L. *The bell stops.*
Mr Frank *turns to the others, making a reassuring gesture, then starts
down the stair-well.*

Effects Cue 39

The bell begins another long peal. Dussel *comes down and
follows Mr Frank out.* Peter *follows after Dussel. The bell stops.*
Mrs Frank, *watching them go, moves to* R *of the table.* Margot
moves to Mrs Frank and takes her hand. Mrs Van Daan *stands up*
C. Mr Van Daan *comes down the attic stairs to* L *of Mrs Van Daan.
There is a motionless silence, then* Dussel *comes up the stairs with*
Peter *close behind.*

Effects Cue 40

The bell starts clanging again. As Dussel *gets a step into the
room, he slumps to his knees.* Peter *helps him to his feet. Shaking off
Peter's help,* Dussel *crosses below the table, goes into the room* R *and
starts packing. The bell stops.*

Effects Cue 41

From far below, we hear a door being battered down. Mr Frank
*returns, bolting the door behind him. The door below crashes. There is
the sound of booted footsteps, then another door is battered down. The
others look to* Mr Frank *as he stops at the head of the stair-well. He
makes a gesture that tells all. A moan escapes* Mrs Van Daan *and
she sags.* Peter *and* Mr Van Daan *go to* Mrs Van Daan *and
help her to the stool up* R. Mrs Frank *sinks down into the chair* R *of
the table and rests her head forward on the tablecloth.* Margot *clings
to the back of the chair.* Mr Frank *moves quickly towards the shelves
up* L, *then stops, turns and speaks to the others)*

Mr Frank. For the past two years we have lived in fear. Now
we can live in hope. (*He picks up a leatherette shopping bag and
Anne's school bag from under the shelves. Moving quickly he gives the
school bag to Anne. The other he gives to Margot and in pantomime asks
her where Mrs Frank's bag is*)

(MARGOT *indicates the W.C.* MR FRANK *goes into the W.C.*

Effects Cue 42

A pair of boots clump heavily up a flight of stairs to the office below. They sound very near. MR VAN DAAN *starts upstairs to pack.* PETER *moves to Anne and kisses her good-bye, then crossing behind her, he goes into the room* L *to pack.* MARGOT *goes up* L *to collect her things.*

Effects Cue 43

The door buzzer sounds. There is a short pause, followed by another insistent buzz. MR FRANK *comes from the W.C. He carries a bag which he gives to Mrs Frank. He then stands* R *of her, holding her hand.* MRS FRANK *raises her head.*

Effects Cue 44

A rifle butt crashes heavily into the bolted door below. With greater and greater violence the blows fall. Shouted commands are heard)

MEN'S VOICES (*off*) Auf machen! Da drinnen! Auf machen! Schnell! Schnell! Schnell! etc. etc.

(MR *and* MRS FRANK *look over at* ANNE, *who stands, holding her school satchel, looking back at them with a soft reassuring smile. She is no longer a child, but a woman with courage to meet whatever lies ahead.*

Lighting Cue 58

The LIGHTS *dim to* BLACK-OUT *except for a spot focused on Anne.*

Lighting Cue 59

The spotlight fades.

Effects Cue 45

We hear a mighty crash as the door is shattered. After a second ANNE'S VOICE *is heard)*

ANNE'S VOICE. And so it seems our stay here is over. They are waiting for us now. They've allowed us five minutes to get our things. We can each take a bag and whatever it will hold of clothing. Nothing else. So, dear Diary, that means I must leave you behind. Good-bye for a while. P.S. Please, please, Miep, or Mr Kraler, or anyone else. If you should find this diary will you please keep it safe for me, because some day I hope . . . (*Her voice stops abruptly)*

(*There is a silence.*

Lighting Cue 60

The LIGHTS *come slowly up)*

Scene 5

Scene—*The same. November 1945. Late afternoon*

When the Lights *come up, the rooms are as we saw them at the beginning of the play, except that the chairs and table are upright, and there is a lamp without a shade on the table* R. Kraler *has joined* Miep *and* Mr Frank. *We see a great change in* Mr Frank. *He is calm, now. His bitterness is gone. Coffee cups are on the table for Kraler and Miep.* Kraler *sits below the table, on the stool.* Miep *is seated* R *of the table.* Mr Frank *is seated on the couch, with the diary in his hands. His coffee cup is on the table* R.

Effects Cue 46

The sounds of the street organ and children at play are heard. The naked bulb in the lamp begins to glow and the scene lights fade up slowly around this lead. When full, we can see it is early evening. The lighting is cool, save the small area around the naked bulb. Mr Frank *slowly turns a few pages of the diary. They are blank.*

Mr Frank. No more. (*He closes the diary and puts it on the couch beside him*)

Miep. I'd gone to the country to find food. When I got back the block was surrounded by police.

Kraler. We made it our business to learn how they knew. It was the thief—the thief who told them. (*He indicates to Miep that she should refill the cups*)

(Miep *rises, goes to the draining-board and collects the coffee-pot*)

Mr Frank (*after a pause; quietly and simply*)   It seems strange to say this, that anyone could be happy in a concentration camp. But Anne was happy in the camp in Holland where they first took us. After two years of being shut up in these rooms, she could be out—out in the sunshine and the fresh air that she loved.

Miep (*moving down* RC)   A little more?

(Mr Frank *does not really hear Miep. After a moment he realizes what she has said*)

Mr Frank. Yes, thank you.

(Miep *pours coffee for Mr Frank, then refills her own and Kraler's cups, returns the pot to the draining-board and resumes her seat* R *of the table*)

The news of the war was good. The British and Americans were sweeping through France. We felt sure that they would get to us in time. In September we were told that we were to be shipped to Poland—the men to one camp. The women to another. I was sent to Auschwitz. They went to Belsen. In January we were freed, the few of us who were left. The war wasn't yet over, so it took us a long time to get home. We'd be sent here and there behind the lines where we'd be safe. Each time our train would stop—at a siding, or a crossing—we'd all get out and go from group to group. "Where were you?" "Were you at Belsen?" "At Buchenwald?" "At Mathausen?" "Is it possible that you knew my wife?" "Did you ever see my husband? My son? My daughter?" That's how I found out about my wife's death—of Margot, the Van Daans, Peter—Dussel. But Anne—I still hoped. (*He picks up the diary*) Yesterday I went to Rotterdam. I'd heard of a woman there. She'd been in Belsen with Anne—I know, now. (*He opens the diary and turns the pages back to find a certain passage*)

(*As* Mr Frank *finds the page we hear* Anne's Voice)

Anne's Voice. In spite of everything, I still believe that people are really good at heart.

Mr Frank. She puts me to shame.

Lighting Cue 61

The Lights *dim slowly to* Black-Out. Mr Frank *slowly closes the diary as—*

the Curtain *falls*

FURNITURE AND PROPERTY LIST

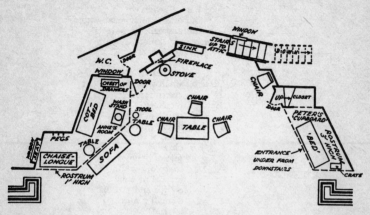

ACT I

SCENE 1

On stage—Centre room: table C, upset
chair R of table, upset
chair up L, upset
chair down L, upset
small table R
stool above table R
chair above stair-well
tattered drape pulled onstage up L
drape up R drawn to conceal sink
tear piece on sofa
sheet in sofa, half pulled out, also pillow
glove on floor by table R
scarf hanging above door L
old curtain on window up C
pallet bed concealed under stairs up L
stove in front of fireplace
pin-flags for war map on mantelpiece
lamp on mantelpiece
sink with running water
dish-cloth hanging on water pipe
2-burner gas plate
tea towel hung on leg of gas plate
empty saucepan on stove
On sink: empty coffee-pot
cup and saucer
glass
mixing bowl
wooden spoon
On shelf over sink: 5 glasses

93

                    paring knife
                    box of matches
                    lid
                    kettle
                    canister of flour

saucepan hanging L of sink
Under sink: 2 pieces of dark bread
            bag of baked potatoes
            bag of beans
            bucket to catch waste water
            dummy grocery parcels
Hanging under sink: skillet
               funnel
               pot
               ladle
On shelves up L: small wash-tub for cat
            electric iron
            8 glasses
            bottle of cognac
            torch, practical
            pack of cards
            chess set
            pile of linen
            spare dish-cloth
            crossword book
            9 cups and saucers
            8 small plates
            mirror
            8 napkins
            8 napkin rings
            8 knives and forks
            cake knife
            cigarette box with 2 cigarettes and box
              of matches
            packet of papers, letters and notes
            Anne's diary, old one
            20 bottles assorted medicines
            4 large bars white soap
            tablecloth
Carpet beater hanging by shelves
Table-lamp concealed behind sofa
Blue knitting on chair above stair-well
Kettle on stove
Room L: mattress on door supported by two boxes
On bed: ticking
        sheet
        blanket
        ticking cover
pictures on wall
concealed in orange crate: bottle of orange juice
                  bottle opener
                  2 glasses
                  cup of water
                  comb
                  mirror
                  shoe-brush
                  pencils in small brown jug
                  crossword book
                  towel
concealed on floor: pillow

                           10 books
                           dictionary
                           saucer
              On shelf: dead plant
                           goose-neck lamp
              black-out curtain at base of skylight
              empty rucksack hanging in closet
Attic room: bed made up with sheet and blanket
              orange crate
              box used as stool
              chair with back removed
              barrel
              pack of cards
              needlepoint frame, yarn and needle
              3 paper-wrapped parcels
              cloth for cleaning fur coat
              newspaper
Room R: sofa, with sheet and blanket concealed
         bed, made up with ticking, sheet, blanket and ticking cover
         small cabinette under bed
         blackout curtains in place over window
         10 books in window-seat
         pair of socks on window-seat
         sewing basket on small box shelf. *In it:* needle and thread
                                            over-sized   bras-
                                               sière
                                            pair of white gloves
         chest of drawers. *On it:* 3 books
                                   scissors
                        In top drawer: pillow
                        In bottom drawer: comb and brush
         round low footstool at foot of sofa
         low cut-off box to complete length of sofa for sleeping
         iron washstand-dresser. *On it:* oval mirror, lying face down
                                          small manicure set
                                          book
                                          hair ribbon
                                          newspaper
                             Under it: large cabinette
              On floor by washstand: lamp, concealed

Off stage—Small rucksack (MR FRANK)

Personal—MIEP: silver cross

SCENE 2

Strike—Rucksack and diary
        Blue knitting
        Ticking on bed L
        Pictures from room L
        Dead plant
        Ticking on bed R
        Torn curtains

Set—Table-lamp on table R
      Table-lamp on dressing-table R
      Undamaged curtains

Move mixing bowl to shelf L

Set up furniture: Armchair to R of table
                  Upright chair to L of table

Off stage—Small cardboard box. *In it:* clippings of cinema stars, photograph of
                    Queen Wilhelmina, diary (MR FRANK)
        2 brief-cases (KRALER)
        Straw bag. *In it:* clothes, comb, hair brush, stockings (MIEP)
        Leatherette hold-all (MARGOT)
        Large brown paper bag. *In it:* food parcels, flask of milk (MARGOT)
        Leatherette shopping bag (MRS FRANK)
        School bag (ANNE)
        Several small bottles of medicine (KRALER)
        Carrier. *In it:* cat with leash (PETER)
        Small plant (PETER)
        Hat-box (MRS VAN DAAN)
        Small straw carry-all (MRS VAN DAAN)
        Paper-wrapped parcel (MRS VAN DAAN)

Personal—KRALER: hearing aid, watch
        MR FRANK: watch, fountain pen
        PETER: penknife
        MR VAN DAAN: cigarette, watch

SCENE 3

Clear centre table

Strike—Thermos bottle

Set—*On table* R: pipe, knitting
    On sink: glass of milk, beans, pot
    On mantelpiece: map
    On table C: 2 composition books, 2 pencils
    Behind stove: bread basket
    On dressing-table R: lesson book, 2 pencils, 2 shopping lists
    At sink: apron
    On window-seat L: stack of books
    In front of table: Anne's shoes, Peter's shoes

Move upstage chair to above table
Open dividing curtains
Table-lamp R, on

Off stage—Brief-case. *In it:* a quart bottle of milk, 2 cabbages, loaf of bread
                (KRALER)
        Brief-case, shopping bag, small medicine kit (DUSSEL)

SCENE 4

Set—Shawl on chair R of table
    Pallet bed up L for Margot

Open couch for sleeping and set bedding
Move stool above stove
Clear table C
Draw curtain up L

Personal—MR VAN DAAN: matches

SCENE 5

Strike—Pallet bed
    Lampshade from table-lamp R

Make up couch bed
Clear everything from table C
Clear everything from table R
Move table C to front of sofa
Move table R to upstage end of table in front of sofa
Move stool from room R to downstage end of sofa
Set armchair above table

Set upright chair L of table
Set armchair L of table
Set footstool L of table

Make up beds in rooms R and L

Set—On tables in front of sofa: white cloth
                                 water pitcher
                                 plate of tarts
                                 dish of walnuts
                                 prayer-book
                                 Menorah with candles
                                 decanter of wine
                                 dish of sliced apples
                                 2 boxes of matches
      In room R: hat lampshade
                satchel with gifts:
                     wrapped used crossword book tagged with poem
                     bottle of home-made shampoo wrapped in paper
                     2 home-made cigarettes in large box
                     envelope containing I.O.U.
                     poorly made knitted muffler
                     ball of paper with ribbon and silver bells
                     used safety razor
                     2 capsules in small box

ACT II

SCENE 1

Strike—Everything from tables R
        Gifts

Re-set furniture with armchair down L

Set—Clothes line with laundry
     On armchair down L: book
     On table C: diary and pen
     On couch: knitted scarf, blanket, shawl
     On draining-board: filled teapot, 8 cups
     On dressing-table in room R: pair of frayed trousers, scissors, manicure set
                                   papers
     On shelves up L: purse with money
     On chest in room R: glass of water

Off stage—Bunch of flowers (MIEP)
                 Shopping bag with parcels of food wrapped in newspaper (MIEP)
                 Bunch of flowers (KRALER)
                 Box of candy wrapped in newspaper (KRALER)
                 Books (MR FRANK)
                 Plate with cake (MR FRANK)

SCENE 2

Strike—Cake and plates
       Blanket from sofa
       Book from chair down R
       Papers from floor of room R

Set—Photographs in room L
     On table C: magazine, ledger, paper, pencil
     On chair down L: glove and needle
     Under mirror in room R: 4 books
      Scarf on hook up L

Replace brush and comb on dresser in room R
Transfer shawl from couch to dresser in room R
Move stool below table

SCENE 3

Strike—Ledger
    4 books under mirror in room R

Clear table C
Move stool to stove
Make up couch for sleeping
Close curtain up L

Set—Pallet bed up L
    On chair R of table: shawl

Off stage—Bunch of flowers (MIEP)

SCENE 4

Strike—Pallet bed
    Everything from table C

Set—*On table:* diary, pen, copybooks, pencil
    On couch: book, 2 pillows
    Stool below table
    Stool at sink
    On draining-board: potatoes, saucepan, knife

Make up couch

SCENE 5

Set scene as at the end of Act I Scene 1
Table upright C. *On it:* 2 coffee cups
Chair above table
Stool below table

Set—*On table R:* lamp without shade, coffee cup, diary
    On draining-board: pot of coffee

LIGHTING PLOT

Property Fittings Required—4 table-lamps, pendant with opaque shade, pendant with heavy shade, goose-neck lamp, wall-bracket

Interior. A composite set of rooms. The same scene throughout
THE APPARENT SOURCES OF LIGHT ARE—skylights, a table-lamp and pendant R, a table-lamp C, a pendant C, a goose-neck lamp L, a wall-bracket in the attic back C, and a light behind W.C. window up R

ACT I SCENE 1 Late afternoon in November

Pre-set to open: Effect of last fading rays of sun through the skylight

Cue 1 *Bring up lights as pre-set*

Cue 2 *Dim all lights to* BLACK-OUT *except spot on Mr Frank and Miep*

Cue 3 *Fade spot on Mr Frank and Miep*

Cue 4 *Slowly bring up lights for Scene 2. Daylight effect*

ACT I SCENE 2 Early morning

Cue 5 *Snap in pendant* R

Cue 6 *Snap out pendant* R

Cue 7 *Dim all lights to* BLACK-OUT *except spot on Anne*

Cue 8 *Fade spot on Anne*

Cue 9 *Slowly bring up lights for Scene 3. Early evening effect. Table-lamp* R, *on*

ACT I SCENE 3 Early evening

Cue 10 *Snap in W.C. light*

Cue 11 *Snap out table-lamp* R

Cue 12 *Snap out W.C. light*

Cue 13 *Snap in table-lamp* R

Cue 14 *Snap in attic light*

Cue 15 *Snap out attic light*

Cue 16 *Snap in pendant* R

Cue 17 *Quick dim to* BLACK-OUT, *except for spot on Anne and Dussel*

Cue 18 *Quick fade of spot*

Cue 19 *Slowly bring up lights for Scene 4. Night effect*

ACT I SCENE 4 Midnight

Cue 20 *Snap in pendant* R

Cue 21 *Snap in centre pendant*

Cue 22 *Snap in table-lamp* L

Cue 23 *Snap in attic light*

Cue 24 *Snap in table-lamp* C

Cue 25 *Snap out lamp* L

Cue 26 *Snap out pendant* C

Cue 27 *Snap out attic light*

Cue 28 *Snap out table-lamp* R

Cue 29   *Snap out pendant* R
Cue 30   *Quick dim to* BLACK-OUT
Cue 31   *Slowly bring up lights in Scene 5. Night effect. Pendant* C, *and lamp* R, *on*

ACT I SCENE 5 Night
Cue 32   *Snap out table-lamp* C
Cue 33   *Snap out pendant* C
Cue 34   *Snap in table-lamp* C
Cue 35   *Slight dim for candle blow-out*
Cue 36   *Slow dim of all lights to* BLACK-OUT

ACT II SCENE 1 Late afternoon
Cue 37   *Bring up spot on Anne*
Cue 38   *Follow previous cue with general lighting*
Cue 39   *Fade spot on Anne*
Cue 40   *Snap in W.C. light*
Cue 41   *Snap in pendant* R
Cue 42   *Dim all lights to* BLACK-OUT *except for a spot on Dussel*
Cue 43   *Dim out spot on Dussel*
Cue 44   *Slowly bring up lights for Scene 2. Evening effect. All fittings on, except W.C. light*

ACT II SCENE 2 Evening
Cue 45   *Snap out pendant* R
Cue 46   *Slow general dim of lights covering the room* C
Cue 47   *Snap on W.C. light*
Cue 48   *Snap out W.C. light*
Cue 49   *Snap on W.C. light*
Cue 50   *Dim all lights to* BLACK-OUT
Cue 51   *Slowly bring up lights for Scene 3. Night effect*

ACT II SCENE 3 Night
Cue 52   *Snap on pendant* C
Cue 53   *Snap on W.C. light*
Cue 54   *Snap out W.C. light*
Cue 55   *Dim all lights to* BLACK-OUT *except for a spot on the group*
Cue 56   *Fade spot*
Cue 57   *Bring up lights for Scene 4. Afternoon effect. Table-lamp* R, *on*

ACT II SCENE 4 Afternoon
Cue 58   *Dim all lights to* BLACK-OUT *except for a spot on Anne*
Cue 59   *Fade spot*
Cue 60   *Bring up lights for Scene 5. Late afternoon effect. Table-lamp* R, *on*

ACT II SCENE 5 Late afternoon
To open: Lights as at the end of Act I, Scene 1
Cue 61   *Dim all lights to* BLACK-OUT

EFFECTS PLOT

ACT I

SCENE 1

Cue 1   *Carillon chimes the hour*

Cue 2   *Carillon fades*
Sounds of distant ships' sirens

Cue 3   *Clock chimes 6 o'clock*

Cue 4   *Street organ and children singing a gay song as they play*

Cue 5   *Sound of distant ships' sirens*

SCENE 2

Cue 6   *Carillon chimes three quarters*

Cue 7   *Sound of marching feet*

Cue 8   *Sound of children playing*

Cue 9   *The carillon sounds and the clock chimes 8*

SCENE 3

Cue 10   *Sound of traffic and ships' sirens*

Cue 11   *Sound of a car arriving and stopping, then driving away*

Cue 12   *Sound of aircraft and ack-ack fire*

Cue 12a   *Fade sound of aircraft and ack-ack fire*

Cue 13   *Sound of buzzer*

Cue 14   *Sound of a streetcar*

Cue 15   *Sound of marching feet*

Cue 16   *Sound of street organ*

SCENE 4

Cue 17   *Sound of drunks singing*

Cue 18   *Sound of running feet*

Cue 19   *Sound of running feet*

Cue 20   *Sound of planes and ack-ack fire*

Cue 20a   *Fade planes and ack-ack fire*

SCENE 5

Cue 21   *Sound of streetcar passing*

Cue 22   *Sound of dog barking*

Cue 23   *Sound of a loud crash*

Cue 24   *Sound of dog barking*

Cue 25   *Sound of feet running downstairs*

ACT II

Scene 1

Cue 26   *The carillon chimes a hymn*
Cue 27   *Sound of buzzer*
Cue 28   *The carillon fades*
Cue 29   *Sound of a marching band*
Cue 29a   *The band fades*
Cue 30   *The telephone rings*

Scene 2

Cue 31   *Sound of children playing*
Cue 31a   *Fade sound of children*
Cue 32   *The carillon sounds and the clock chimes 9*

Scene 3

Cue 33   *Sound of buzzer*

Scene 4

Cue 34   *Sound of Military Band playing Viennese waltzes*
Cue 35   *The telephone rings*
Cue 35a   *Stop telephone*
Cue 36   *Sound of a car arriving and stopping*
Cue 37   *Sound of a car arriving and stopping*
Cue 38   *Clanging of electric bell*
Cue 39   *Clanging of electric bell*
Cue 40   *Clanging of electric bell*
Cue 41   *Breaking of doors and booted footsteps*
Cue 42   *Sound of heavy footsteps*
Cue 43   *Sound of door buzzer*
Cue 44   *Battering of door*
Cue 45   *Crash of door breaking*

Scene 5

Cue 46   *Sound of street organ and children playing*

COSTUME PLOT

MR FRANK

ACT I SCENE 1

To open: Pink shirt, black tie, trousers, waistcoat, old brown overcoat with scarf, socks, loafers

During Scene: Put on muffler

During Black-Out: Remove overcoat with scarf, muffler
      Put on hat, jacket with star, new overcoat with star

ACT I SCENE 2

During Scene: Remove hat, overcoat, loafers

During Black-Out: Remove jacket with star
      Put on grey sweater

ACT I SCENE 3

During Scene: Put on loafers

During Black-Out: Remove sweater, waistcoat, loafers
      Put on pyjamas, slippers

ACT I SCENE 4

During Scene: Put on new overcoat (*star removed*)

During Black-Out: Remove overcoat, pyjamas
      Put on jacket (*star removed*), hat

ACT I SCENE 5

During Scene: Take off hat

ACT II SCENE 1

To open: Brown shirt, blue tie, large trousers, large waistcoat with watch and chain, sweater, loafers

During Black-Out: Remove sweater, loafers
      Put on tweed jacket, slippers

ACT II SCENE 2

During Black-Out: Remove tweed jacket, waistcoat
      Put on pyjamas

ACT II SCENE 3

During Scene: Put on overcoat

During Black-Out: Remove overcoat, pyjamas, slippers
      Put on tweed jacket, loafers

ACT II SCENE 4

During Black-Out: Remove tweed jacket
      Put on old overcoat with scarf, muffler

ANNE

ACT I SCENE 2

To open: Beret, pink blouse with star, grey skirt, cape, gloves, 4 pairs panties, red sweater with star, white sweater, grey stockings, shoes

During Scene: Remove gloves, 2 sweaters, cape, 3 pairs panties, shoes, star from
   blouse
During Black-Out: Put on red sweater

ACT I   SCENE 3

During Scene: Put on shoes, hair bow
   Put on and take off Peter's cap, trousers and jacket; Mrs Van
   Daan's coat
During Black-Out: Remove bow, blouse, skirt, shoes, stockings, red sweater
   Put on nightgown

ACT I   SCENE 4

During Black-Out: Remove nightgown
   Put on red dress, beige stockings, shoes

ACT II   SCENE 1

To open: Slip, yellow sweater, green skirt, shoes (*no stockings*)
During Black-Out: Remove skirt, sweater

ACT II   SCENE 2

During Scene: Put on blue blouse, blue skirt, white gloves, pink shawl, Margot's
   shoes
During Black-Out: Remove shawl, blouse, gloves, shoes
   Put on nightgown, blue sweater

ACT II   SCENE 3

During Scene: Put on green skirt used as make-shift cape
During Black-Out: Remove nightgown
   Put on shoes

MRS FRANK

ACT I   SCENE 2

To open: Blouse, jacket, skirt, jabot, red sweater, nightgown over above, over-
   coat over all, shoes, grey stockings
   Carried: bag, hat, gloves
During Scene: Remove jacket, jabot, nightgown, overcoat, sweater
During Black-Out: Remove shoes

ACT I   SCENE 3

During Scene: Put on shoes, apron
During Black-Out: Remove blouse, skirt, shoes, apron
   Put on green dress, nightgown

ACT I   SCENE 4

During Scene: Put on and take off pink shawl
During Black-Out: Remove nightgown
   Put on shoes, lace shawl, ear-rings and necklace

ACT I   SCENE 5

During Scene: Remove shoes

ACT II SCENE 1
To open: Old large blouse, old large skirt, old large jacket, small jabot, gloves
with fingers cut off

During Scene: Remove gloves

During Black-Out: Remove jacket, jabot

ACT II SCENE 2
During Black-Out: Remove shoes, blouse
Put on nightgown

ACT II SCENE 3
During Scene: Put on pink shawl

During Black-Out: Remove nightgown
Put on pink blouse, shoes

MARGOT

ACT I SCENE 2
To open: Yellow shirt, green skirt, yellow sweater, pink nightgown, purple
skirt, grey cotton stockings (*worn throughout the play*), shoes, coat,
green hat, gloves and belt in pocket of coat

During Scene: Remove hat, gloves, coat, purple skirt, nightgown, yellow sweater,
dress

During Black-Out: Roll up shirt sleeves ·

ACT I SCENE 3
During Scene: Put on shoes, apron

During Black-Out: Remove apron, shoes, shirt, skirt
Put on nightgown, slippers

ACT I SCENE 4
During Scene: Put on dressing-gown
Remove (*behind curtain*) nightgown, slippers
Put on pink jersey top, purple skirt, ear-rings, shoes

During Black-Out: No change

ACT I SCENE 5
During Scene: Remove shoes

ACT II SCENE 1
To open: Purple skirt, lavender shirt with sleeves rolled, wine skirt, yellow
sweater, Mrs Frank's red sweater, pink stole, muffler

During Black-Out: Remove stole, muffler, red sweater
Put on shoes to fit Anne

ACT II SCENE 2
During Scene: Remove shoes for Anne
Put on slippers

During Black-Out: Remove yellow sweater, wine skirt
Put on nightgown

ACT II SCENE 3
During Scene: Put on dressing-gown

During Black-Out: Remove dressing-gown, nightgown, slippers
           Put on shoes

MR VAN DAAN
    ACT I SCENE 2

To open: Padding, vest, shirt, tie, trousers, jacket with star, shoes, socks, waist-coat, overcoat, gloves, hat. Underdressed: shirt and tie. Concealed between waistcoat and jacket: shirt and sweater

During Scene: Remove overcoat, hat, gloves, shoes, waistcoat, shirt, sweater, jacket
           Put on jacket

During Black-Out: Remove star from jacket
           Put on shoes

    ACT I SCENE 3

During Black-Out: Remove jacket, shirt and tie, shoes

    ACT I SCENE 4

During Black-Out: Put on shirt and tie, jacket with handkerchief in pocket, waistcoat, shoes, hat

    ACT I SCENE 5

During Scene: Take off hat

    ACT II SCENE 1

To open: Large shirt, large trousers, sweater, gloves, slippers
           Remove padding

During Black-Out: Remove sweater

    ACT II SCENE 2

During Black-Out: Remove shirt, slippers

    ACT II SCENE 3

During Black-Out: Put on shirt, jacket

MRS VAN DAAN
    ACT I SCENE 2

To open: Blouse, skirt, jacket, fur coat, hat, gloves, bag, shoes, stockings, bed-jacket, apron

During Scene: Remove apron, bed-jacket, fur coat, gloves

During Black-Out: Remove jacket, shoes
           Put on jabot

    ACT I SCENE 3

During Scene: Put on shoes

During Black-Out: Remove shoes
           Put on nightgown, slippers

    ACT I SCENE 4

During Scene: Remove slippers, nightgown, jabot, blouse, skirt
           Put on gold evening dress

During Black-Out: No change

ACT I   SCENE 5
During Scene: Remove shoes

ACT II   SCENE 1
To open: Large blouse, large skirt, slippers, Peter's raincoat, scarf
During Black-Out: Remove raincoat, scarf

ACT II   SCENE 2
During Scene: Put on apron
During Black-Out: Remove apron
               Put on nightgown

ACT II   SCENE 3
During Scene: Put on blanket from sofa as makeshift cape
During Black-Out: Remove nightgown
               Put on jacket, apron

PETER
ACT I   SCENE 2
To open: Black shoes, brown stockings, pyjama trousers, new trousers, belt, old trousers tied around waist, brown knickers, new blue shirt, bow tie, new blue sweater with star, waistcoat with star, new jacket with star, raincoat, cap
During Scene: Remove waistcoat, jacket, raincoat, jacket, star from sweater, old trousers
During Black-Out: Remove knickers, shoes, sweater

ACT I   SCENE 3
During Scene: Put on shoes
During Black-Out: Remove tie, shoes, trousers
               Put on dressing-gown, slippers

ACT I   SCENE 4
During Black-Out: Remove dressing-gown, slippers
               Put on trousers, shoes, blue tie, waistcoat, old jacket, cap

ACT I   SCENE 5
During Scene: Remove cap, shoes

ACT II   SCENE 1
To open: Black shoes, brown stockings, old trousers, belt, pyjama trousers, padding, old blue shirt, tie, old sweater, old jacket, wool cap
During Black-Out: Remove jacket, tie, sweater
               Put on red tie, waistcoat, jacket

ACT II   SCENE 2
During Black-Out: Remove tie, waistcoat, trousers, shirt, padding

ACT II   SCENE 3
During Scene: Put on shirt, trousers, slippers
During Black-Out: Remove shirt
               Put on sweater

DUSSEL

(*Pre-set in W.C.:* jacket, quick-change tie, dentist's coat without star, green sweater, slippers)

ACT I SCENE 3

To open: Sweat shirt, pyjamas with handkerchief in pocket, black shoes, socks, new grey shirt, tie, new pants, dentist's coat with star, trench coat, hat

During Black-Out: Strip to pyjamas

(*Transfer everything to W.C. to pre-set for Act I Scene 5*)

ACT I SCENE 4

No change

ACT I SCENE 5

To open: Jacket, quick tie, shirt, shoes, socks

(*After Act I Scene 5 set:* jacket in room R, shoes in W.C. and 1st Act dentist's coat and tie in dressing-room)

ACT II SCENE 1

To open: Old shirt, tie, old trousers, slippers, socks, Mr Frank's overcoat

During Black-Out: Remove overcoat, slippers
                    Put on dentist's coat without star, shoes

ACT II SCENE 2

During Black-Out: Remove shoes, dentist's coat
                    Put on slippers, pyjamas

ACT II SCENE 3

During Scene: Put on jacket

During Black-Out: Remove pyjamas, jacket
                    Put on green sweater

MIEP

ACT I SCENE 1

To open: Underdressed: blue skirt, 2 sweaters, collar. Purple skirt, baby padding, hat, shoes, grey stockings, shortie coat

During Black-Out: Remove coat, skirt, padding, hat

ACT II SCENE 1

To open: Scarf, long coat, green skirt, green blouse, hat, gloves

ACT II SCENE 2

During Black-Out: Remove scarf, long coat, green skirt, green blouse, hat, gloves
                    Put on nightgown, scarf, trench coat (*as worn by Dussel in Act I Scene 3*)

ACT II SCENE 5

To open: Purple skirt, baby padding, hat, shoes, grey stockings, shortie coat, matron's blouse

KRALER

ACT I SCENE 2

To open: Brown jacket, waistcoat, shirt, tie, trousers, shoes, socks

ACT I SCENE 3

To open: As Scene 2 but change tie

ACT II SCENE 1

To open: As previous Act plus overcoat. Change tie

ACT II SCENE 5

To open: As Act II Scene 1; carry hat

"HANUKKAH"

YIDDISH FOLK SONG